EARNED
My Journey to Becoming A Hunter of Man

Robert Terkla

With New York Times Bestselling Author
Nicholas Irving

ISBN: 978-0-9997697-8-2

CONTENTS

A Child's Innocence

The field to a sniper is like his safe haven. A sniper should feel comfortable in nature, understand her. Where some tremble when venturing into the darkness of the woods, a sniper is at peace. Over my time in sniper school, and after that, I adapted to the environment. I was able to manipulate it to empower me like an artist is enabled by his brushes.

The field became a tool for me that I could use when needed. It took decades before I was able to see open nature the way I do today. Deep inside, whenever I ventured into woods, there was always a sickness in the pit of my stomach.

I've always been opened to discussing my past. There are some topics I was at first uncomfortable talking about, but over time I did. Then, there are some topics I felt if I exposed to the public, it would somehow hurt me. I wasn't sure how to discuss something that once hurt me and could hurt me again. My mind simply chose to forget about specific events and move on. Like how the brain works after a combat deployment. The activities that occur in that hellish environment are sometimes too harsh a reality to face. And instead of living with the daily thought of those events, you seemingly forget about them.

No matter how long rotten memories are kept under a mental lock and key, the stench is still there. Over time, that stench can seep out, and you begin to recognize its smell. Sometimes the smell can become so overpowering, making you sick and affects who you are.

It doesn't take a war to experience the harshness's life can offer. Some experience it long before they can serve in the military. For me, I was introduced to a life-altering experience in the same places I would find comfort as a sniper…the woods. I was seven or eight years old at the time, living in our home in Washington. My parents were still together at the time, and life wasn't so bad. I lived like any other kid would at that age.

Playing outside until the sunset with the neighborhood kids wasn't out of the normal.

My younger sister and I would get into the occasional arguments and fights and made up the same day. The only care in the world was looking forward to long summer breaks. The area around my home was surrounded with large twenty-foot tall trees and brush. In the summer, if you wanted to find the kids, they'd be in there playing kid games and having a good time. At that time, the woods were our safe haven. Our neighbors in our neighborhood never caused any issues as far as what I could tell. What anyone would expect of the typical middle-class families in the nineties.

Our secret

"You have to make sure this is our secret between the two of us. We wouldn't want anyone finding out about our hiding spot, right?" The older man said to me. His baritone, grumbly voice made it hard for him to whisper.

The sun was starting to set, and I knew that my mom would be asking for me if I wasn't inside.

"Okay." I hesitantly responded as we exited the woods.

I wasn't sure what he meant or why we need to have a secret. Our secret wasn't something that I was familiar with, and my dad never talked about these secrets. A square wooden pallet on the ground, concealed by berry bushes and brush marked where the man and I had been. My mom was making one of my family's favorite go-to meals on

Thursday afternoon, spaghetti with meat sauce.

The walk to my house was a short walk, less than five minutes. The man who had accompanied me stayed behind as for a minute or two after I left him. His actions struck me as odd as to why he would stay back as he lived next door to me. Maybe he forgot something in our secret spot? Perhaps he noticed how close it was to the walking trail and needed to better hide our secret spot.

Walking in the front door of my house and I was greeted by my mom, serving up a hot plate for me. My dad and sister were both at the table, waiting for me to join the family.

"Where were you, Drew? Didn't see you out back." My dad said. Drew is the nickname my dad called me as a kid.

I was hesitant to respond at first, knowing I had a secret to keep. But there still was that strange sickening feeling that sat in my soul. The type of sickness that makes your insides feel like they're being dropped from the Eiffel tower. I was to the point that keeping a secret made me want to vomit.

"Oh, Jimmy and I stopped by his house to grab his water gun," I responded with my head down, staring at the steam rising from my plate. I never made it a habit to lie to my dad. My parents raised my sister and me with good morals. My mom would remind us time to time that good morals made a person rich, not what they have to show. As hard as it was to tell a fib, it was as hard not to break a promise.

"Well, you need to be home earlier next time and make sure you keep an eye out for your sister." She said.

It was hard for me to take a bite of food. Usually, a hot plate of spaghetti after a long day's play, my mom would have reminded me to chew. This meal felt different, however. The secret that the man next door and I had kept playing back in mind. Looking at the plate of food and listening to my family eat were like nails on a chalkboard to me.

Every bone in my body wanted to say at least something, but I couldn't. I was too scared of what might happen to my neighbor if I broke our secret. The secret that I kept inside was more of an experience, and the longer it replayed in my young mind, the more it confused me. Being able to form the words I needed, to share what I knew felt impossible to forge.

Nothing was said throughout our family dinner. The conversation shifted to my younger sister, and the attention was on her. A part of me wonders if my off demeanor raised any alarms. Alerting my parents that something more that evening happened. My parents knew Jimmy's family well and would only have to ask if they felt I was lying. Some of me wishes that they did ask Jimmy's mom and realized I hadn't been with him.

I would continue to see the man, my neighbor, at various times throughout the week. Some days he would meet me as I was walking along the sidewalk to meet up with friends. He would make sure that when he approached me, no one was around. After meeting my older neighbor, he suggested visiting our secret spot. This scattered pattern of meetings on a small pallet in the woods went on for months. In the early nineties, from what I recall, times were relatively safe. Where I lived, it was common to leave the front door unlocked overnight. After school, kids walked home unsupervised for half a mile. My parents had never worried about anything happening in our small community. The only way anyone would know something foul was going on was to speak up.

I thought my prayers would finally be answered on one of the secret meetings. Sounds of snapping branches approaching us froze the man still. My shirt was off laying on the ground next to me. I wanted to reach down, grab my shirt, and run towards the noise. I knew what I heard were the sounds of someone walking.

"Shhhh." The man whispered as he placed his index finger over his lips. I remember the fear he had in his eyes as he stared at me. It was the first time that I had the opportunity to see someone who was as scared as me. His belt was unstrapped around his worn, dirty blue jeans.

The closer the footsteps came, the more the urge I got to jump up and run. No matter how much I wanted to run, my legs froze. I could hear the thump of my heart beating in my eardrums sitting there like a statue. The footsteps came within twenty feet from us. A narrow walking path paralleled us that had little foot traffic. The trail was rarely used, and the grass and weeds were starting to grow over it. The brush that covered the small clearing I was in was just enough to remain hidden.

As quickly as the footsteps approached, they faded further into the distance. The beating thud of heart went silent as it dropped to my stomach. I couldn't see who the person was wandering in the woods. At the time, I tried shrugging it off as an animal or something. Thinking to myself, if it were a person, they would have seen us. However, I knew it indeed was a person. Someone who could have taken me home to my parents, where I knew I would be safe.

I became a loner child over those terrifying months I held the secret. Instead of going outside to play, I stayed in my room. The comfort of my small ten by fifteen-foot room became my safe haven throughout the day. Staying inside would, at the least, guarantee I wouldn't see our next-door neighbor. I would rather sacrifice summer months locked in my room than live through another traumatizing event.

My parents never questioned why I stopped playing outside. The quiet, secluded kid that began shying away from conversations seemed to not bother them. Nightmares became more intense and vivid each night. Images that I unintentionally blocked from my mind played back as I slept.

The constant fear of the man next door climbing into my window at night as I slept, taking me away, kept me awake.

It would take the courageous actions of my younger sister to save me from the hell I was in. Being the older brother, I never would have thought she would be my protector. I was supposed to be her older brother, the one who is the protector. If she ever had an issue or someone were to bully her, I would have her back. The day my sister spoke up when she knew something was wrong, is a moment I'll hold forever.

Free

"Mommy! Mommy!" My sister's blood-curdling scream was ear piercing as she shouted, running through the front door.

"The man next to us touched me in a private parts mommy!"

My sisters' words were barley manageable to understand. I could hear the trembling in fear in her voice as she tried explaining what happened to her. I could tell by the look in her eyes what she was trying to say. It was the same look of fear that my sister had in her eyes I recognized and related to. That same fear that she was now experiencing is what I lived with for months.

Watching her from the open door of my bedroom, explaining to my mom, I felt a mix of emotions rush over me. As a big brother, I felt like I let her down. I should have been there for her when my sister needed me the most. Another part of me felt as if a huge truck was lifted from my shoulders. It was if the secret itself could be weighed on a scale, after being surgically removed from me.

Emily cried in my mom's arms while she held her on the living room sofa.

"Has Tom done something to you too, Drew? I'm not mad at you, and you can tell me." My mom said. She saw me out of the corner of her eye, standing in the doorway, peering in to listen. She tried asking me as calm as she could while trying to mask the anger in her voice. My mom wasn't mad at Emily or me. As a caring mother, it was instinctual for her to be outraged. I know all my mom wanted to do was kill the neighbor next door.

Because of my sister, I was able to speak up. The burdens of being ashamed, worried, and scared were lifted.

"Yes, ma'am," I responded loud enough to barely be heard. I felt ashamed that it had taken so long to say something. Seeing how much it hurt my mom hurt me just as much.

My dad, who was sitting in his favorite chair at the dinner table, listening in spoke up.

"That son of a bitch is a dead man!" My dad said as he gnawed his teeth. My father was always the quiet one. For him to raise his voice and curse in front of us was rare.

My dad grabbed an old wooden baseball bat, kept by the front door and stormed out. I wasn't sure what my dad was going to do to the man or his intentions. It was the first time I saw my dad infuriated to the point of an altercation. My mom stayed on the couch with my sister consoling her, rocking her back and forth. "It's not your fault, sweetie. It's not your fault." She repeated to her over and over.

I could hear my dad pounding on Tom's screen door through my bedroom window. My dad shouted for a few minutes persuading Tom to come outside before he did. Tom, an older man in his forties, single, no kids of his own, usually stayed to himself. He moved into his property a couple of years before my parents moved in. He didn't stand out or draw attention to himself. His estate was well kept, and he washed his car from time to time on weekends.

I continued to listen through my window as my dad berated him. There weren't any sounds of a scuffle or screams of help.

"I ever catch you around my kids again, and I'll beat you with this bat, you understand me, Tom!" My dad yelled before coming back to our home.

Nothing was the same for some time after that night. My dad slammed the door behind him as he came inside and went to his room. Emily fell asleep in my mom's arms as they laid on the couch. All our lives took a dramatic shift, and we didn't know how to deal with it. My family was ordinarily able to talk to one another. I could always go to my dad if ever something was wrong, as well as my sister.

The topic that night that needed to be addressed never was. Instead, it was put under a large rug in the center of our family. An open conversation that my family needed slowly became a large boulder we all avoided. Time in a sense, moved on as nothing happened. Average conversations among us gradually became less uncomfortable over time. No matter how much we tried to ignore it, we all hurt. A secret that I kept for so long was now out, only to become a secret we stayed within our household. My parents didn't call the cops or file some form of complaint. The topic of child molestation was a taboo topic during those times. Sexual abuse was and still is the fastest-growing form of abuse reported involving children.

Despite the abuse's uptrend, it was rare to hear stories like the one my sister and I experienced. For some reason or another, the topic to this day seems to remain mostly unaddressed. The innocence of a child taken away in seconds with lifelong implications, occurring in record numbers and not a word?

My sister and I wouldn't see or hear from our neighbor after my dad approached him. He was too ashamed to want to show his face in public. The coward he was more than likely thought the word reached the rest of the neighborhood. Not that I tried to see him or care about him after that. It was as if he disappeared, tucking himself in his small home to rot.

While the experience of that short, terrible period of my life happened decades ago, it still affects me to the present day. Who I became after that, changed me in a way yet to grasp. Venturing into the woods and the way I viewed them changed. The natural beauty and life that I once saw became revolting. The smell of dead leaves that littered the ground were nauseating.

I didn't know if the person I was to become or where life would lead me. Becoming a hunter of man, most comfortable surrounded by the brush, would be my most trying hurdle to overcome.

<u>Dad</u>

"You will and can do everything that you put your mind on." My aunt, Tracy, said to me, sitting on my front porch. Not knowing what to say to me after my dad's death, she spoke these words as best she could to make me feel better.

My aunt and the last words my father spoke to me before passing has remained with me every day since. Tracy was the only family member who had regularly attended treatments with my dad. I didn't know it at the time, my dad was battling cancer and kept it a secret from me. If it weren't for my aunt, I'm not sure where I would be in life. A soft-spoken lady, my aunts' words of encouragement pulled me through some of my darkest times.

I rarely talk about my dad, although I find myself thinking about him more often. When I do remember my dad, no matter how pleasing the memory, it's shattered by the few hours I saw him alive.

My girlfriend at the time, Sarah, was wrapping up her trip out to see me. During her visit, I thought it would be the perfect time for her to meet my dad. On the way to pick Sarah up from her hotel, I decided to pay my dad a visit first. It was Sarah's last day in town, and I wanted to make sure the two of them finally met. I was on somewhat of a time crunch and couldn't stay at my dad's house long, but I wanted to let him know Sarah, and I would be on the way.

My dad lived at a small townhouse by himself, close to downtown Seattle after my parents divorced. Opening his front door and looking down a hallway leading to his bathroom, I saw my dad's figure standing over the sink. Not overthinking it, I invited myself inside and walked towards him.

"Hey, old man!" I shouted.

I could see him from behind, standing over the sink and thought maybe he hadn't heard me. It wasn't until I could hear him spitting and coughing into the sink did, I realize something was wrong.

"Dad?" I said, running over to him.

"Yeah, I'm good. Just give me a second. I had grape juice earlier, and it must've been bad, that's all." He responded.

I looked down over his shoulder into the sink as he vomited into the sink again. The odd purple color that I saw filling the bowl, at first didn't register to me. My dad's entire appearance suddenly seemed to change in front of my eyes. His stomach was bloated to the point where it looked like it had been inflated with air. His feet were swollen to the point that his socks began cutting the circulation to his legs.

My dad had some prior issues and never really made a big deal about them. I guess that's one way you could describe my dad. He was stuck in his old school ways when it came to hospital visits. If there was something wrong with him, he felt that he was the only one who could take care of and deal with it. There had to be a dire emergency before my dad would consider seeing a doctor. The image of what he thought a man should be, sometimes got in his own way. My father was the type of guy who generally kept to himself and a man of few words. He wasn't the type to beat around the bush and would always give it to you straight.

That night, as my dad threw up in the bathroom sink, he knew that wasn't one of those times he could try and brush off. Regardless of him saying that it had been grape juice, I knew otherwise. His words began to slur and became unintelligible. A fog of confusion and fear covered his eyes.

My Aunt Tracy, being one of the closest relatives that I have, was who I immediately called. I wasn't sure exactly what to tell her without scaring her and cause her to panic.

"Hey, Tracey. Dad's not doing so well. I just walked into his house, and I saw him throwing up in the sink. He says it's nothing, but I think he may need to see somebody." I said to her over the phone.

I moved my dad to his bedroom and sat him on the foot of his bed to try and catch his breath. My aunt Tracy didn't want to make the drive alone, so she brought her sister, Cindy, with her.

I sat and stayed with my dad in his bedroom until my aunts arrived an hour later. The three of us carried my dad to the car and drove him to the hospital less than a fifteen-minute drive away. My aunts tried to remain as calm as possible as to not worry me. Neither one of them seemed as if things were as bad as they were while Tracy rested my father's head in her lap. No matter the calm demeanor they displayed, I knew they were as concerned as I was.

The memories of that night, playback in my mind like snapshots and lapses of time spread about. When we arrived at the hospital, those portions of time begin to fade. I remember hectic nurses and doctors rushing over to my dad and placing him on a gurney.

"Make sure Sarah gets to the airport and catch her flight." My dad, mustering up what strength he had left said to me.

They were also the last words I would hear from my dad, as well. He knew Sarah was flying out that night. Being the guy he was, he didn't want to be the reason I was late taking her to the airport. Little did he know that after that flight, Sarah would later become my wife and mother of my amazing daughter.

I went on to see Sarah and left my dad to the care of the doctors that evening. A few days passed before I paid him a visit in the hospital. Somewhere within that short period, I learned that my dad had fallen into a coma and was unresponsive. My grandmother, who was now at my dad's side, said that I should come over to see him.

Arriving at the hospital that evening became one of the most traumatizing events of my life. Now, having seen the harsh realities of war, nothing can compare to witnessing my dad's last moments alive. War, put mildly, is pure hell. There are things in combat you may observe, that will haunt you for the rest of your life. Then, for me, there is the moment I saw my hero, my dad, evaporite in front of your eyes. In combat, I found ways to numb myself and could disconnect from the chaos of war.

My family packed into a small hospital room with a curtain divider, now all stood around my dad's bedside. Hooked up and connected to plastic tubes and wires, he started showing signs of hope. His eyes slowly began opening. He wasn't looking at anyone or thing. Instead, his eyes wandered as if he had no control over them.

The room fell silent, dropping a feather in the room would have shattered the silence. The beeping sounds and alarms from the hospital equipment were drowned out in our disbelief. It took my dad a few seconds before his eyes fully opened. As he looked around the room, it looked as if the whites of his eyes were painted over. A yellow hue blanketed them as if mustard was injected into each eye. Discoloring of the eyes is one of the effects of liver failure, known as Jaundice. A condition the whites of the eyes yellow due to high levels of bile fluid secreted by the liver.

I think we all knew that was going to be the last time we would see my dad alive. His eyes twitched back and forth as if the muscles and nerves in his eyes had lost control of themselves. Seeing my dad in such a vulnerable state shocked me to the core. It's one of those moments in my life that when I look back, it results in sleepless nights. A moment for me, I rarely share with anyone outside of those who were there.

My grandmother, being the consoler that she was, took me and brought me out of the room. She knew that wasn't the way my dad would have wanted me to see him. He would want me to keep the good memories of him that I had and hold them the closest.

My family and I stayed at the hospital that night and slept when we could in the waiting room. My dad held on and fought, I'm sure as long and as hard as he could. However, his battle with cancer eventually came to an end. Less than twenty-four hours later, one of the doctors walked into the lobby to give us the news.

I'm not sure what the doctors' exact words were to my grandmother as she informed her of the loss of her son. I do remember the scream she let out, and the pain in her voice echoing against the walls. A cry that I will never forget and hope I never experience again.

Life without my dad in my life was a hard concept for me to grasp. I was angry, I regretted not spending more time with him, sorrow in not being able to be there for him. Emptiness, resentment, and countless other emotions are overwhelmed at once. Regardless of the faults and shortcomings, my dad had in his life, his loss shook to me my core.

I became cold inside to where I could physically feel the chill, mourning his passing. It changed my emotions and feelings about life. The life I had in view ahead of me seemed empty and dark from that point on. There wasn't some idea that I could bounce off my dad if I needed advice. Stopping by randomly, my dad's place to say high was now only as real as my memory allowed. I was alone in the world, and I could care less about what it had in store for me.

While my dad was alive, he brought up the idea about his funeral once or twice. He mentioned not having the typical casket and ceremony funeral. My dad knew he could save our family a third of the cost by getting cremated instead. The value of the dollar was never overestimated in our household. We lived by a penny saved, is a penny earned. Adding financial stress on the family if he passed was the last thing my father would want.

I was the only pallbearer carrying my dads remain at his funeral. My mom and sister both decided not to attend or say their last goodbyes. I was, in fact, one of the few family members to show up. Regardless of who chose to participate in the funeral or not, I refused to hold negativity towards them. After all, my mom and dad were both separated, and my mom was seeing someone at the time.

I wouldn't revisit my dad for some time, over a decade after placing him in his resting place. I felt like a coward up until that point. Having taken so long, so many years as my life went on, not going back to see him. By then, I married Sarah and had a daughter, my military career had come and gone. I was finally establishing my place in society, by the time I went to his grave. Visiting my dad after all those years finally brought me closure. A closure I not only needed but benefitted from.

After all those years, I realized how much my dad taught me, regardless of our short time together. He showed me life sometimes deals you a bad hand occasionally. Like a gamble at a Las Vegas casino, you don't have a choice in the hands we're dealt with. No matter a good or lousy deck of cards, the game will be played to the end. There's no point in complaining about a terrible situation, you just play with what you have.

Youth

Being a kid, while your parents are separating, can be one of the most challenging experiences to have. If you've never experienced a divorce or a parental separation, be thankful. My parents separated during my teenage years, between the ages of fourteen and fifteen. Throughout and after their divorce, I experienced emotional, physical, and physiological stress. I changed as an individual as opposed to the person I was when my family was together.

A child typically externalizes the problems caused by the separation of their parents. Impulsive behavior, rebellion, and conflict amongst their peers are some ways a child can display their problems. While these are only a few of the 'symptoms' a kid may face, I recall experiencing them all.

My childhood leading up to my parents' divorce was just like any young boy. You know, the typical behavior almost all little boys have. Making friends, playing outside, getting into a bit of mischief here and there, and the occasional neighborhood scuffle over immature disagreements. My parents never displayed any struggles that we were going through as a family, or at least that I could see.

If my parents were having any financial issues, my sister and I have no memory of it.

As most parents did and did back then, they masked economic hard times. The mindset they were raised in was all about making the best with what they had. As kids, we didn't have anything to compare our lifestyles to. The kids who lived in our community all went through the same struggles as I did. To us, there were never signs of a struggle or out of the normal. As far as we were concerned as kids, we had it made. We didn't have the latest video games or phones to keep us entertained. If we wanted to see what our friends were up to, we went to their house.

The house that I grew up in was in the rainy state of Washington and was far from extravagant. A single, one-story residence less than two thousand square feet living space and shared among four of us. After owning my own home now, I realize how small our house had been. My room shared with my sister for a few years was a ten by twenty-foot space. Our house had two bathrooms, a small kitchen that leads into our family room, and a large yard. In comparison, my home was around the average size of today's trailer home.

I'm not saying that what I grew up in was the worst place to live because it wasn't. It also wasn't a place I would want to raise my family today. But it was home, and it still holds a childhood worth of memories in it. It was the place where I learned to play catch, throw a football, ride a bike, and enjoyed the friendships made. My home was the melting pot that would begin to mold the man I am today.

My hometown was relatively small, less than fifty thousand residents made up our community. Both of my parents worked small jobs to make ends meet, sometimes multiple.

They tried everything that they could at the time to keep things together. Regardless of their issues, their intent was never to have a fall fate to a failed marriage. I guess a fear of theirs was, that by separating meant ruining the lives of my sister and me.

After years of trying to keep the strings of their marriage together. The tension between the two of them eventually snapped. I wasn't sure at the time what exactly happened or who placed blame on who. Time seemed to be moving at light speed in the confused mind of a thirteen-year-old.

The months leading up to my parent's divorce, my dad found a place of his own and moved out. Daily arguments between the two of them reached a point living together caused more harm than good. There wasn't a need to try and uphold a façade of a perfect family for my sister and me. Besides, we were all walking on eggshells leading up to my dad's departure. No one knew what to say to each other, not knowing if it would cause drama.

Whatever the issue was between them, he was always man enough to admit his faults and accept the consequences. My dad, I believe, always kept a special place in his heart for mom, and it showed from time to time. My dad deciding to move out was the type of thing I would have expected him to do.

While my dad was in the process of moving, it forced my sister and me into an uncomfortable situation. Both of us had to decide as to which parent we would want to live with. My mom wanted my sister and me to stay and live with her. She felt that it would interfere with our schooling if we moved to another side of town. The stress during the divorce was enough.

Choosing between my mom and dad

was one of the hardest decisions that I ever had to make. I loved both of my parents just as equally. My decision came down to the last minute before my dad walked out the door for his last time. The connection and influence my dad had on me, lead to my decision to move in and stay with him. My dad and I moved to a small, single trailer home that was closer to town. I never had anything against my mom as a kid or held resentment toward her. Living with my dad was what I felt I needed at the time. The only happiness and comfort I could find at that time were being with my father.

Living with my dad during the first few months was relatively stress-free. My dad spent most of the day working long hours and into the night. Before catching the school bus in the morning, my dad would still be asleep after working a graveyard shift. After school, I had the house to myself, and I wouldn't see him until I was about to go to sleep.

I took the new freedom and responsibility and handled it with care. I didn't have a younger sibling to watch after or entertain, only myself. The added responsibility gave me my first taste as to what it felt like to be a man. The emotional toll the divorce took on me, I bottled inside. Bringing up how I felt, I thought, would only add to my problems, I believed. Some nights I found myself waking up covered in sweats, occasionally having night terrors regarding my parents' breakup. In my dreams, I was responsible for their falling out.

Throughout the first year, making as well of the situation as I could, I eventually began slipping. The crowd I started to hang around with had an influence on me. Not having the oversight of a parent around, my friends became my guardian. The older guys I would hang out with became my influencers. My outward actions and those I hung around with were a representation of how I felt. Continuing my rebelliousness, I found myself smoking and selling marijuana. I was introduced to smoking and drugs before I was able to obtain a license.

Drinking and smoking didn't come cheap, and I didn't have a job to sustain my growing addiction. Stealing a few bucks from my dad's wallet here and there, supplied my cravings for only so long. Instead of going out and getting a job like a normal fifteen-year-old, I found other means of making income. On one such occasion, I went as low as to selling my Xbox to buy an ounce of weed. I tried to sell it to who I thought was a legit drug dealer but ended up being a gang member. Instead of getting the bad of weed, I was given a black eye, and he got away with a free game console.

This hole I was falling down, seemed to have no end and grew darker as time passed. Smoking and drinking took the last bit of desire out of me to stay in school, and my grades started to fall. The days that I did attend consisted of me too incoherent to learn. The anger that I knew how to hide so well became less manageable, causing me to become confrontational. A school brawl during and after school was the expression of my emotions. Ultimately, I felt that it was best to drop out during my high school sophomore year. Showing up to school with no motivation to learn and fighting wasn't worth it. I felt that I was going through enough in my life.

My dad knew of some of the dangerous and illegal activities that I was getting into.

Completely eliminating the odors of alcohol, tobacco, and the distinctive fragrance of a skunk often associated with marijuana is nearly an impossible task. It struck me odd, however, that my dad never gave it too much attention to my behavior. The proper scolding and ass whipping that I needed never came. I figured that my dad was either too tired or didn't care to punish me. Any other time, my dad would have sent me packing the way I was misbehaving.

My changing personality and who I was becoming, furthered the distance between my dad. I was basically living under his roof, destroying my life, and getting away scot-free. I know all my dad wanted was to kick me out for the way that I was acting. Knowing how much I depended on the relationship he and I shared in the past, I don't think he could bring himself to kick me out.

Days would elapse without my dad and me being under the same roof at times. I was intoxicated much of the day and would crash out at a friend's house. That was my routine. The average day I would wake up sporadically in the afternoon hours, still hungover from the night before. Before wiping the sleep from my eyes, I'd smoke a terrible tasting, used joint, then wash it down with a warm beer. Later in the day and into the night, I would drink some more, then head downtown to cause trouble. Instead of walking or catching a ride back home, I would crash on a friend's sofa and wake up to repeat the cycle. Days turned into weeks, and the weeks turned into months, the sequence of my dangerous way of living continued.

My dad never had the opportunity to kick me out of his place. The two of us hadn't seen each other in so long, it was like I wasn't even there. By then, I was used to taking care of myself without my dad or mom around. I essentially kicked myself out and moved into a small apartment with two older females, Ashley and Mary. I met the two of them through one of my good friends of four years and has always had my back. The two of them were both trying to hang onto a college career and part-time jobs. Ashley and Mary were both nineteen years old at the time I moved in with them. Both high school friends who grew up in Washington, not too far from where I was from. After graduating, they were able to afford a small two-bedroom apartment while attending the local college.

The three of us all came from divorced families. We were also all forced to decide what parent we would live with over the other. What we had in common made us gravitate towards one another, and we understood one another. A few of the guys I was friends with thought I had it made, living with Ashley and Mary. However, there was never any funny business between the girls and me. To Mary and Ashley, I was like their little brother. They took care of me and made sure I always had a place to sleep at night. Sure, I lied and went along with the fantasy the guys threw around, but I was only wanting to fit in with the group. The way the guys looked up to me, like I was their teenage hero, in a way felt good at times.

While the fantasy of living with Ashley and Mary was there, my reality differed drastically. My bad habits were only facilitated and encouraged. The young man that I was becoming would have disappointed my mom and dad. My entire upbringing as a child, my parents did their best to stray my sister and me away from drugs and mischief. The bad traits I developed would have landed me in serious trouble if they got word of what I was getting into. In a way, my doing the most extreme was my way of crying out, without screaming out loud.

I had plenty of wake-up calls and opportunities to change the course I was on. For example, the time I found myself in a car with illegal substances and open containers of alcohol. Out one night downtown, my roommates, Mary and Ashley, decided to meet up with some of their friends. None of us had anything in mind other than hangout. The night was supposed to be one of our chill nights. Mary and Ashley had a small party at the apartment the night before, and we were strapped for cash. We had enough money to grab a bite to eat and get back to our place.

After meeting with Mary and Ashley's friends, we decided to eat at a local fast food spot. I knew a shortcut that cut between two buildings and was a straight shot from where we were and led the pack. The area downtown we were in, was known to be a party spot, and the nightlife could get crazy at times.

Leading the way through one of the back alleyways, someone in our group noticed a laptop inside a car, sitting in plain view. On crowded party nights, cars are usually parked in alleys to avoid parking fees. One of the guys in our group pulled on the driver's side door to see if it were unlocked. I didn't know who he was, other than my roommates were friends with him or knew of him. I felt that no matter how far I tried to stray away from trouble, it always had its way of finding me.

The rest of the group ended up serving as his lookout while he opened the car door. I should've spoken up then, but I was too scared to say anything. Mary noticed that the keys were sitting on the floorboard and told her friend to grab them. The peer pressure now had been enough to push the situation over the edge. Before I knew it, we were all piling into the car and starting the engine. Caught up in the pressure and moblike mentality, not wanting to be the oddball, I joined in. We weren't going to take the car to a chop shop or commit any crimes other than the one we just committed. Our plan was to drive the car around for a few blocks and park it. The laptop was the only item that Ashley and Mary's friend was interested in and could cash in at a pawnshop.

There were six of us total crammed in a silver and black, a small four-door coupe with less than a quarter tank gas in it. I could tell that the driver was either hungover or drunk. He didn't have any problems as he drove over the speed limit and swerved in and out of lanes passing cars without a signal. In downtown Washington, where there's plenty of drunk drivers at night, there were sure to be cops somewhere.

"Shit, shit, shit!" Mary suddenly said. She was sitting behind the driver's seat and on top of Ashley's lap. Looking out the back-corner window of the car, she saw a cop pull in behind us and start tailing.

"Dude, chill! Everybody just calm down, we're not doing anything. I'm going to pull into a gas station, and we'll get out and be alright."

The police cars blue and red lights filled the inside of our car like a Christmas tree. The police car behind us chirped his siren and instructed us to pull to the side of the road over his loud horn.

"I knew it..." I said aloud. My initial plan for making a run for it evaporated as quickly as they came.

I knew that if I ran, I could only make matters worse. There was no outrunning the cops at that point. We were caught red-handed, and all I could do was hope I could somehow talk my way out of it. I also knew I shouldn't have been in the situation, to begin with.

The cop pulled us to the side of a two-lane street under a streetlight near a bar. Everyone in the car remained silent, hoping the cop wouldn't run the license plates. A bright flashlight beam shined into the driver's side windows, blinding us as the cop approached.

"Dude, I have weed on me." The driver said under his breath, leaving none of us time to react.

The cop was now standing at the driver's door, I knew all of us were going to jail. I couldn't afford bail and had no one to call to help get me out. Instead of freaking out, I decided to accept the consequences that I knew were coming.

Tap, tap, tap. The police officer tapped his knuckle on the window and asked the driver to roll the windows down. "Where are you all headed in such a hurry?" The officer said. "You guys look like you're headed to somewhere important the way I saw you driving down there." He continued.

"Uh, uh, we're going back to our place. I'm dropping off my friends, sir." The driver answered, keeping his hands on the steering wheel. There was a long pause and silence as the officer continued scanning his flashlight beam in the car. I thought the officer may have caught the odor of marijuana through the open window.

"You kids be a little more careful. I

know it's getting late, and you guys all want to make it home, correct?" The officer unexpectedly said after a call came in over his radio.

"Yes, sir." The driver cautiously and hesitantly responded.

To our dismay, the officer decided to only give us a warning. If only he ran the car plates, he would have seen we were more than innocent teens trying to make it home safe.

Once the officer got back to his car and pulled away, we ditched the car in its spot. All the contents inside the vehicle were left inside. We figured we used up all the luck we were allotted that night and decided to split our separate ways.

My life seemed to continue its downward trajectory. I moved around from one part-time job to another throughout the town. The longest and the last position that I held was at a small convenience store. The hours were flexible, and I didn't have to work the weekends. I would save up a week's worth of pay and use that for food and booze.

I worked as a bagger for a few months before moving to the shopping cart retriever. It wasn't a job I wanted to keep in hopes of making it career. I was paid an under the table salary, and a high school dropout. Mom and pop shops were the only establishments willing to hire me at the time. The freedom I once had was now occupied with the dreaded responsibilities of having a job. Every other day was the same routine, just as before. The only difference was I wasn't always under the influence. To make some money, I had to be somewhat coherent. When the shopping cart ben was full, I went out and brought the carts inside and placed them in single-file rows. At the end of my six-hour shift, the store manager would pay me in cash.

As much as the work became rudimentary and showing up to work became a job, being there is what changed my life. Standing outside of the store on one of my shifts, an army recruiter gave me the idea to join the army. A recruiter, dressed in the army dress uniform, wearing polished black boots, was passing through our side of town. It was rare to see military uniforms as far as we were from any military installations.

The recruiter saw and approached me, asking if I ever gave joining the army any consideration. At first, I wanted to brush him off and end the conversation before the sales pitch. Looking at the pins and medals on his chest instead, sparked my curiosity.

"I mean, I have once or twice." I said, knowing that if I showed the slightest interest, he would continue.

I was ready for a change in my life. The path I was on only had one outcome for me. Meeting the recruiter on that day was the key to unlock the box I put myself in. A short ten-minute conversation elapsed, and the recruiter had my contact information.

It took a few months before I would sign the line of my army contract. Being a high school dropout put a delay on my recruiting process. The army required that I at least held the equivalent of a diploma, and I initially didn't qualify. However, with the help and tutoring from my recruiter, I received my G.E.D.

Two weeks after receiving my mail in diploma, I left for basic training. I didn't put in for a two-week notice or tell my mom or dad. I just left. I wanted to get out of Washington as fast as possible. Throwing away all the bad I experienced in it and leaving them behind. I made it up to this point on my own, and I didn't need anyone's help where I was going.

It Has Begun

It's official—day one of week one in the US Army's sniper school. I've had a few weeks of training getting familiar with my rifle and some sniper terminology while I was in the pre sniper course. The military's need for snipers was increasing during the years I was in the army. This demand for snipers forced units to conduct a pre sniper school for guys wanting to try out. Due to the military spending budgets, these pre-courses increased the odds of their men graduating. Basically, it boiled down to Uncle Sam, getting a good return on its investment. Afterall, sniper school has a history of failing seventy to seventy-five percent of those who attend. Those who do successfully navigate the eight-week course will earn the right to call themselves snipers, a hunter of man.

I was fresh off a deployment when I decided to put in for my sniper packet. The first step into becoming a sniper is filling the necessary admin paperwork and medical exams. During that time in my military career, I was full gung ho. I felt that I could go after anything and take on the hardest tasks and schools the army had to offer. I was already thinking about trying out for the Green Berets. After sniper school, I planned on trying out for the special forces selection process if all went well.

Combat can do that to some of the guys, make them want to take on the world. After a good deployment and all your brothers in arms are back home safely, you damn near feel invincible. Not just being deployed to a combat zone, but to be fully immersed and engage with it. Having come out on the other side of war, it made me feel as if I could do anything. Compared to my life two years ago, in Washington, combat had been the highlight in my life.

I've had the itch of going to sniper school for some time, and this deployment was what I needed to scratch it. I remember asking my platoon leader about sniper school our first day back to work stateside. Without much thought, he had no issue sending me and signing off on the paperwork. It's not that I wasn't some stellar soldier or did anything special to have my commander give me the green light. In fact, I rarely outscored my peers on physical fitness tests. While I could shoot, I wasn't the best shooter in my platoon of fifty men. I was okay, however, at following directions and doing the job at hand until its complete.

You don't have to be the most badass, ultimate shooter to become a sniper. For the most part, it just takes an open mind willing to learn and then being able to apply it. But, there are some traits that a unit commander may look for in sending someone to sniper school. For instance, having a good moral standing with your peers in your unit is a must. The guys in your squad must have trust in you because, as a sniper, you'll be covering their backs. Those who outrank you must also trust you with the lives of their men. Your commander will also want to make sure that you have leadership characteristics that can be built upon.

I was physically in shape after deployment and had no issues passing the physical fitness portion. To attend sniper school, you must be able to pass the standard army physical test, APFT. Pushups, sit-ups, a two-mile run, and pull-ups. While sniper school doesn't come across as being physically challenging, you'd be surprised in what a three-hour stalk can take out of you.

I told Sarah that I was going to give sniper school a shot after I had all my ducks in order with my unit. She knew the type of person I was long before the Army, and I loved a challenge every so often. Sarah knew that I could be as stubborn as they come at times. When I put my mind on something, I got it done or die, trying to make sure I gave all in the process. Sniper school was no different. Sarah always supported me with what I did, no matter how out of left-field the idea was. No matter how extreme my life ventures may come across or take me, Sarah has always been my greatest supporter.

While in sniper school, I would be away from home and Sarah for a little more than eight weeks in total. After nearly a year-long deployment, I'm sure it took a massive toll on her. In the long run, time won't have seemed as long, compared to the lifelong right of being a sniper. Sniper school for me and my career would be worth every sweaty, painful, and nerve-racking moment.

Two weeks before the start date of sniper school, my unit held a pre-sniper course to get us ready. While far from the real school, for the guys who attended with me, the course wasn't taken lightly. Some of the topics discussed in the pre-course familiarized us with shooting equations, distance ranging, and stalking.

While the course tries its best to prepare you for the actual school, nothing truly can prepare you. There isn't some secret program or recipe that can guarantee anyone's success. It boils down to showing up, learning, and performing to the best of your ability.

After getting familiar with how life would be in sniper school, it was finally time to see what I was made of. Ft. Benning Georgia, the home of the infantry soldier, now the maneuver center of excellence, is the birthplace to the army sniper. A military base so big that it has its own zip code. The installation is covered with towering pine trees, airfield drop zones, and runways, massive ranges that can stretch out for miles. In the summer and warm months, the smell of the bases various swamps permeates the air, a telltale sign you're on Benning.

I, along with three other guys from my unit, received our military orders temporarily assigning us to the base while training. My home unit was in Savanah, Georgia, making our trip to Benning a short one. Students coming from outside duty stations drove or had to fly. For us, a road trip a couple hundred miles was freedom that didn't come across too often. Driving in your own vehicle, dressed in the attire that you want to wear, and being away from top brass was like a breath of fresh air.

As refreshing as the breath of freedom was, it was short-lived the moment we arrived at the sniper school headquarters. We arrived early in the morning the day sniper school started. That is at least what we thought according to the orders we received before leaving. It wasn't long until we saw that something was off, rolling my truck into the student parking lot.

The sun barely had time to crest over the tree line. I saw a group of students in uniform, moving with a sense of urgency. If there's anything in the army that stands out more than a sore thumb, it's a bunch of enlisted soldiers running around.

As our luck would have it, it turned out that we had arrived on day 1 of sniper school. Day one was the official start of sniper school, having all students present and accounted for. Everyone else attending the course, they had time to settle in for at least a day or two and had a chance to meet one another. Those who were early, stayed on the training grounds, sleeping in a cabin style barracks. They had time to get familiar with the layout and hear the horror stories from guys who were on their second try.

My guys and I arrived with just enough
time to sprint over to the headquarters office
and check-in. All the clothes and gear for
sniper school remained in the back of my
pickup truck. Throughout my military career
up until this point, I was never late to a
formation or training event. I learned early on
as a new guy in my unit that being late could
be the difference between life or death, in our
line of profession.

Showing up late the first day of sniper
school was one of the most embarrassing
moments in my career. You never want to
ever be "that guy," especially on the first day
in one of the army's few gentleman's courses.
A gentleman's course in the military is a
course that doesn't treat you like a day one
troop in basic training. Gentleman's course or
not, I was still expected to uphold a high
standard—one who is responsible as well as a

soldier who is on time. If trying out for Green Beret selection was something that I wanted to give a shot, I couldn't allow this mistake to become a habit.

"Snipers! I need everyone to the sniper shed time now and grab helmets and something to write with. We have a hard time to be on the trucks that will be parked outside at 0530!" One of the students, the class leader, yelled out to the gathering cluster of sniper students. The class leader's job is disseminating information from the head instructor to the class. Each student, in some way or another, will get a chance to hold a leadership position.

The sniper shed that our class leader was referring to, was a sizeable metallic framed building. Somewhat resembling an old aircraft hangar, emptied out and bare walls. Walking into the front entrance of the sniper shed, are several ghillie suits hanging from the ceiling. It isn't until you get a closer that you see that each one is uniquely designed and labeled each with a class number.

Each ghillie suit, the iconic uniform to the sniper, representative of every class that has graduated. All the ghillies, signed with the names of the men, some old and barely visible with fading ink and black permanent marker. Along the walls of the shed were eight-foot-tall wall lockers and long, plastic collapsible tables.

The instructors didn't leave much time for us to talk, but I did have time to figure out what I walked into day one. I asked one of the students what I had missed and learned that we were heading out to qualify by shooting in. Shooting in is a sniper's first right of passage in becoming a sniper. Each sniper solidifies his right to remain in the course, by being able to demonstrate their ability to shoot.

During pre-sniper, each candidate had to qualify expert, using a stock M4 without the aid of scope or red dot sight. A good ole bare naked rifle with old fashioned iron sights. The goal of shooting in, is to demonstrate an understanding of the fundamentals of shooting. A target with a sheet of paper is placed twenty-five yards in front of each shooter. On each target, is the silhouette of a human torso measuring only a few inches in size. Each shooter must place five bullets within that silhouette to qualify and move on with training. The pattern of holes produced by bullets punching on the paper downrange is called a shot group. If the grouping can fit within a three-inch circumference, you're good to go. Having the ability to do so, a shooter must have a sound understanding of the basics. It's the job of the sniper school instructor to take those fundamentals and mold them into the tools of precision.

Shooting a target twenty-five yards away wasn't a task I would typically be too concerned about. However, a lack of sleep, a long day's drive, and a bladder full of caffeine did. Shooting for me, was a lot like taking the APFT, army physical fitness test, in the army. Before the fitness test, I would get a few days' heads up and had time to prep. Jumping into a task headfirst without any preparation or notice always rattled me, mainly when my fate relied on it.

There were around sixty of us in total, and the mood amongst the class was relatively relaxed given. There were a few Marines and SEALs and a couple of air force guys as well. The Navy and Marines stood out like a fish out of water, marked by sporting long hair and relaxed surfer attitudes. They kept to themselves for the most part but were never afraid to remind you who they were.

The range we were heading to was a ten-minute drive from the sniper school shed. Plenty of time to go over in my head the fundamentals and settle in. I even tried to close my eyes and get a minute or two to rest them before shooting. The only thing preventing me was the bumpy ride and hard wooden seats inside a two and a half-ton truck from World War 2.

"Alright, gentlemen, welcome to Day one sniper school. This will be your first evolution, and I will be giving you your task, conditions, and standards that will be expected of you." A tall sergeant wearing a black ball cap shouted. The class enthusiastically piled out of the back of the trucks as we arrived at the range, ready to shoot. It was my first real encounter with the instructors of sniper school. All the instructors at sniper school stood out by their difference in uniform. Instructors wore black ball caps with the coveted sniper symbol sewn in on the front.

The instructors didn't have to scream at the tops of their lungs and harass us like they would in basic training. Every student wanted to earn the right to be a sniper and was mature enough to perform the job. The tasks and conditions were what was to be expected of us. Today, the task was to successfully shoot in, the conditions were up to me, and the ability to overcome my own nervousness.

We formed single file lines in rows of ten along the range zero-yard berm. The instructors passed out the M4s we would use, our ammo, and then placed our targets downrange. Once one student was complete in shooting their five rounds, some of the instructors would help grade the results. After each iteration of fire was finished, the cycle would repeat. I was the third shooter to fire in my line. Behind me, Luke Perry, a young E-4 specialist and one of my guys, who drove with me. I didn't know him too well as he wasn't in my platoon. From what I had seen of him in pre-sniper, he was a solid shooter and someone I would have no hesitation backing in a gunfight.

I couldn't tell how the grading was going, but it seemed everyone was breezing through. Less than a minute of shooting per student and the line would advance.

"Next shooter up!" The instructor announced. I was next up to shoot.

Having done this on numerous occasions, I knew the only thing that could get in my way was me. I knew what needed to be done and how to shoot. Hell, I was combat-proven, and allowing five bullets to intimidate me wasn't going to happen.

After shooting, the instructors went out and retrieved our targets and brought them back to see and grade. I could see the sunlight punching through the five holes on the paper target, but my shots were far left of the silhouette by a few inches. My heart started to sink.

"You're shitting me!" I said to myself.

The instructor held out the target in front of me and pulled out a three-inch transparent circle from his chest pocket and placed it over my shot group.

"You're a GO sniper. Go join the rest of the class behind the trucks and prepare to head back to the schoolhouse." He said.

I was confused. My sights were on the target, my breathing was excellent, and my trigger squeeze was as good as it was going to get. Sure, I was a bit tired, but there's no way I should be that far off unless it's the sights. Why am I getting a pass?

"Dude, did you put all of your rounds on target. I was impacting far left, but I still have a GO." I questioned one of the students, an 82nd airborne paratrooper, standing by one of the trucks,

"Yeah." He said, spitting a mouthful of chewing tobacco spit onto the ground. "All of our shots are going to be off. The weapons aren't zeroed at all. They're just making sure we can group within the capabilities of the gun." He continued.

The clarification calmed whatever my worries and concern were. Shooting within the capabilities of the rifle, meant placing five rounds within a prescribed circumference that is designated by the gun. These capabilities are often expressed in minutes of angle or MOA. Simply put, a one MOA shot group is equal to a one-inch diameter shot group at one hundred yards distance. So, at one hundred yards, a one MOA rifle should produce one-inch groupings. A two MOA rifle should hold a two-inch diameter grouping. Three minutes of angle will give you a three-inch group, and so on.

The standard military-issued rifle is, at best, a three MOA rifle. An expert shooter in the military should be able to hold a three-inch grouping at one hundred yards. To do so, having a firm grasp on the shooting fundamentals is what set us up for success. The fundamentals are basic in themselves. They are having a steady firing position, proper breathing, excellent sight picture, and a smooth trigger pull. Having these fundamentals become second nature, shooting the capabilities of the gun shouldn't be an issue.

While day one of sniper school was off to a terrible start, the first test was now behind me. I could now start putting my focus on what needed to be accomplished. The only thing left for me to do was get back and unpack. I had to unload all my gear, grab a bunk, and get some good sleep. I barely had time to call Sarah to let her know that I had made it or how the day went. By the time I settled in and prepared for the next day, the only thing I wanted to do was sleep. Week one of sniper school was officially underway.

Snaps, Movers, Shooters...Oh My!

We were pinned down for hours now on top of a grassy hilltop. I, along with a sniper from my unit, was attached to a SEAL team during my second deployment. We were on a mission operating near a village in the Northern region of Afghanistan. The village had a heavy Taliban presence that harassed the locals regularly. It was our mission to clear that area of the enemy the best way we knew how. Killing them.

I couldn't have asked for a better deployment working alongside special operations. The SEAL team I was attached to were good at their job. Damn good. I never had the slightest hesitation whenever we would head into harm's way, having seen them in action on more than one occasion. The SEALs never strayed from a fight. Their confidence and fearlessness were admirable and contagious, rubbing off on me easily. Clearing out a village running rampant with enemy Taliban fighters wouldn't be a challenge. Surrounded by professionals who are willing to die for you, no mission seems challenging.

We traveled to the target in a dozen or so 4x4 off-road vehicles. They were basically like moon buggies, except they came equipped with heavy machine guns. In the mountains of

Afghanistan, the terrain often determines your means of travel. Large boulders and possible IED, improvised explosive devices, halted our movement and forced our team to travel on foot.

We walked along the base of a valley, surrounded by large building-sized hills to our left and right. It wouldn't take a rocket scientist to see how bad of a position this was for us to be in. Making our movement along the hilltops would silhouette us against the morning skyline. The village was less than a kilometer away, and traversing the hills would set us behind schedule. One grenade or burst from enemy machinegun fire means catastrophe to a group our size.

As we walked the gravel floor bed, we tried our best to remain silent, keeping ten feet between each man. I was near the rear of the formation carrying my SCAR heavy rifle with a ten-power scope. The SCAR is still a relatively new rifle that the army tested for a few years. The new gun is a semi-automatic rifle that fired the standard sniper round, 7.62 M118LR. On a good day, I could reach out and touch a target half a mile away. Anything beyond that, the ballistics and environmentals increase the likelihood of a miss.

I had sniper school under my belt and months of training before deploying. Countless hours of dedicated training and trigger time, it felt good to finally take the ultimate test. I wasn't sure if I would have the opportunity to pull the trigger or not and didn't care. My primary role as a sniper was to support and observe.

SNAP, SNAP, SNAP, Crack!

"Troops in contact!" The SEAL team commander's voice was suddenly heard over our radios.

Less than three hundred yards away from our target when enemy gunfire erupted around us. A SEAL team squad of assaulters immediately returned fire in the direction of the incoming fire. I could feel the rumble and precision of our machine guns bouncing against my chest. Our team quickly split into five, predesignated smaller groups, and began to maneuver into the village. Four teams of four men set up positions around the village entrance. The remaining teams served as the assault team. The assault team's job was to clear the village house by house. In combat, room-clearing takes time and leaves the group vulnerable to enemy forces. It was our job, as support and overwatch, to allow the assault team to carry out their task safely.

Being a sniper, I was positioned on one of the hills along with a few SEALs, overlooking the village. Enemy fire on our positions became relentless at times and went on for hours. The assault team on the ground was fighting through a constant barrage of gunfire as they cleared the area. Unrelenting at times, I recall wondering to myself, how the enemy was able to have so much ammo and where they were able to obtain it.

Communications between the teams spread across four hills were at best mediocre. The rolling Afghan terrain would often cause issues with radios communications. Being on the same page as a team and knowing your job often makes up for the technical difficulties. As the assault team continued to clear the village, so did the gunfight in the hills. The fire became so overwhelming at one point, it allowed the enemy to move closer to our overwatch positions. It remained our job to keep the assault team safe. To do so, we must be able to see our guys and be able to

eliminate threats when presented. The slopes
of the hills that accompany Afghanistan can
make seeing everything around you,
impossible.

During the firefight, the Taliban
managed to maneuver towards the hill next to
the one I was located on. A SEAL on an
adjacent hill saw them and called it over the
radio, drawing my attention, or else I wouldn't
have seen them. The transmission went heard
by all the overwatch positions, except the
team who was in immediate danger.

The quick thinking of one of the
SEALs on the hill with me quickly eliminated
the threat. Eric, a broad-chested country boy
from the south, who stood six foot two, fired
three shots in rapid succession. Three Taliban
fighters wearing blue and white robes
dropped where they were. All three bodies
crumbled atop of each other before slowly

rolling down the hill. The skill and actions of Eric possibly saved the lives of his brothers in arms.

The focus of the enemy firing from multiple hilltops from concealed positions was now focused on us. I guess Eric dropping the three Taliban fighters didn't sit right with their buddies. All hell seemed to break loose around us. I can still recall the thud of the bullets as they smacked the ground a few inches in front of me. The tall grass that once partially aided in our concealment began cutting down by a few inches as incoming fire mowed them down.

With my face pressed into the ground, I managed to catch glimpses of where the enemy fire was coming from. Able to peak my head up a little, in between volleys of gunfire, I spotted bright flashes emitting from the surrounding hills. These cameralike flashes of light marked enemy positions, a few hundred yards away. The fighting style of Afghanistan was what I believe Vietnam must have been like, rarely seeing the enemy. Their guerilla-style tactics were making it harder for us to engage. Rather than engage us head-on, they used ambushes and hid in caves and fought from concealment. Every now and then, I was able to make out the partial shape of a torso, but it lasted only seconds.

The enemy firing on our position didn't seem to be letting up anytime soon. To gain the upper hand, the overwatch teams would have to reposition. While one of the teams moves to a better fighting position, the other provided cover. Once that team was set, another would move into their place while being covered by the set teams. This tactic, known as bounding, would continue until we were able to better engage the enemy.

Laying in the prone while looking through my scope, something in my peripheral caught my attention. To my left, just beyond five hundred yards, a dark blue shadow streaked across the ground. For a split second, I thought nothing of it. Afghanistan isn't the cleanest place on Earth, so it could have been several things. The target detection training that I had in sniper school was the only reason I decided to further investigate.

Shifting my rifle over and aligning my scope to where I saw the glimpse, I noticed its true identity. Through my scope's magnification, I could make out the figure of a man. I could see his blue clothing as well as the AK-47 that he carried with him. He also wasn't alone. Behind him, another fighter in a darker garment carrying the same style rifle. They must have crawled their way to our positions during the initial fire. I knew what their intent was as soon as I saw them try and hide. The enemy fighters were on a mission to intercept and ambush the bounding SEAL team.

Just as they had a goal in mind, so did I. I didn't have time to tell Eric that targets were in my field of view. His focus was on avoiding getting shot while managing to return the hate. My goal was as simple as, kill them before they killed one of us.

The two Taliban fighters stood up and took off on a sprint. I knew their distance and wind speed. A slight breeze on the left side of my cheek meant a left, three-mile an hour wind. The dead sprint of the Taliban would be my main concern. From the kneeling position, I placed the lead fighter in my scope, far ahead of the fighter, and began to squeeze the trigger. I didn't want to aim at my target, if I did so, my bullet would land far behind him.

I wanted him to run into my round as it traveled ahead of him, like meeting in space and time. Anyone familiar with skeet shooting, apply this shooting tactic all the time.

I lead my target using the first few mil dots and fired. A miss! Dirt kicked into the air, where my bullet impacted the ground and quickly dissipated. My elevation was spot on. I needed to give my target more lead by aiming further in front of him. I underestimated his speed as well as the wind and needed to quickly adjust. I fired three more shots, each shot separated by half of a second, time to regain my sight picture to see where I hit. If I were using a bolt action rifle, it could have taken me a second or two to reload and fire.

The fourth shot connected. My target was almost outside the field of view and used all the mil dots in my scope. My 7.62mm round hit with him such force he didn't have time to make an extra stride. A puff of red and pink mist exited his body, the Taliban fighter dropped to his knees and slid face first in the dirt. The remaining fighter who was trailing him saw his buddy and decided to run a different direction. I never had to engage the second target as he went of sight behind a tall bush.

At the time, I didn't overthink the shot or even what it felt like. It was the first time I ever killed another human being. The emotion I thought would be there, never came. I didn't have the luxury to think about how I felt as the firefight continued. The shot itself wasn't anything spectacular, in the moment. I honestly thought it was more luck than skill.

It was years after that engagement when I thought in depth about making the shot. I never took the time to analyze what it took to make it until I wrote my first book, Never Fear Anything. No matter how much luck went into making a shot on a sprinting target, there was some skill. During sniper school, we took a week to hone our skills to hit a moving target. This week is known as Snaps and Movers week.

Day 1 Snaps and Movers

Snaps and movers are a common term used in sniper school. The term refers to moving and limited exposure targets. A snap, a partially exposed target, is a target that presents itself for no more than three seconds. Meaning, a sniper would have a three-second time frame to hit a target at a given distance. Movers, of course, are targets that move and simulate walking laterally to the sniper.

Hitting a moving and limit exposure targets wasn't new to me, or anyone in sniper school. It's something every soldier learns in basic training. In basic, each recruit must be able to qualify the moving target range to graduate. After basic training, many graduates will deploy within six months. You learn fast on your first deployment that humans tend to move a lot. They especially tend to move more so when they're being shot at. The enemies' guerilla warfare tactics can make it seem like fighting ghosts. The amount of time the enemy is exposed to engage is extremely limited. That's why getting familiar beforehand is a skill learned early on.

Sniper school takes those necessary skills and knowledge and builds on them. Hitting a moving target over long distances requires more than being able to aim well. Each sniper must also have a firm understanding of mathematics and physics, along with being a decent shot.

Shooting longer distances means the bullet spends more time flying in the air. If a target is moving and the sniper shoots aiming directly at it, the round will miss its mark. I like to think of it as a quarterback throwing to a receiver. For the receiver to catch the football, the quarterback leads him, throwing ahead of the receiver. Determining exactly how far in front a sniper needs to lead his target, requires a mathematical equation.

Math was never one of my strong points in grade school, and I didn't find it interesting. I would try to hide or skip the math homework I was assigned in grade school. It wasn't until sniper school that I found a new appreciation and love for mathematics. I would never have thought I'd be doing algebraic calculations and the

Pythagorean theorem. Knowing back then that math could be weaponized, perhaps my outlook on school would have been different.

A Snipers Dream

"Roger Sentinel. Cleared for infill to rally point, Yankee. Scorpion Three, Out." Our base commander's voice was garbled, but discernable through my radio earpiece

"We got the green light, Eric, let's roll," I said over to my spotter, who was pulling security a few yards from me.

This was the moment every sniper dreams of. A Hathcock moment is the best I could describe it. Moments when there's no room for collateral damage, and our high-value target of interest was better off dead. The stealth of a sniper team and precision of their rifles are the only tools needed for this mission.

Practicing stalks in sniper school and perfecting the art in hunting man was one thing, but doing it was another. Having that opportunity to display this unique talent on the battlefield is what a sniper's dreams are made of. A sniper can serve out his entire career and never pull the trigger, let alone conduct a live stalk. Getting the green light from our commander, made up for all the blood, sweat, and tears that goes into this craft.

Eric and I were getting our last minute items together. We planned to be at our second checkpoint before sunrise. An eight-mile movement at a cautiously slow pace would take some time. Moving out before sunset would put us on a few hours ahead of schedule. Having the extra time allowed my team to set up our hide sight before the locals got out of bed.

Being the sniper team leader for the mission, it was my job to conduct planning beforehand. The area I decided to take our shot from was five hundred yards from a small Afghan village. Our target, Assad Rashmi, was a high-value target that moved around our area of operations. Our intel showed Rashmi had been the mastermind behind a string of IED attacks in the region. He was also responsible for the most recent series of IED attacks near military bases.

We tracked him down and were able to monitor his movements with predator drones. After observing him for a few weeks, we were able to see a pattern in his actions. While

Rashmi moved around, often sporadically, he returned to one place regularly. Every three weeks, Rashmi made a stop at a small village to harass and collect money from the locals. He and his goons would stick around and receive what they needed, then leave the following early morning.

The money that Rashmi stole from the local villagers would be used to purchase the materials used to make IEDs. His preferred choice of IED, a pressure plate packed with seventy pounds of explosives. Rashmi's IEDs was not only devastating, but they were also becoming the number one cause of casualties' in the area.

In the early years of the war, a drone observing Rashmi could have dropped a bomb on him. Due to political interference and the shift in rules of engagement, collateral damage was unacceptable. Each time a building shook from an explosion nearby, and a villager's door fell, we paid the bill. Instead of giving out large amounts of money for negligible mishaps, the bombing campaign ended.

The shift in the war campaign was felt by every allied force on the ground fighting. The enemy noticed the change, as well. Enemy fighters and leaders became cocky, and their freedom of movement expanded. Without taking our foot fully off the enemy's throat, precision would be the way we had to fight.

While this was my team's first real-world stalk, we were more than ready. Eric, like myself, also had two deployments under his belt. Eric served as a mortarman for his first deployment before switching over to infantry and becoming a sniper. We worked together over a year and could read each like a book. The sniper and spotter bond that we had felt as if it was molded through decades of work.

Our work overseas spoke for itself and the reason my team was chosen for this mission. While I outranked Eric, we both shared a mutual respect for each other's craft. Eric was a great shooter but could outshine me reading the wind on any day of the week. I respected his ability and having him calling my shot, made me a better shooter.

The movement to our checkpoint took us through valleys and deescalated farmlands. Having most of our progress under cover of darkness allowed us a quicker pace. In the last thousand yards, we would have to dawn our ghillie suits and make our final approach to our firing position. I felt that my team could make an eight-hundred-yard shot with my .300 Winchester magnum and wouldn't be an issue. However, getting to a place to take the shot meant traversing open terrain a few hundred yards.

The .300 magnum I used could hit a target out to 1,100 meters. The .300 projectile had a lower drag making it ideal for longer distances. My spotter, Eric, armed with a 5.56 SDM-R. A modified M-16 was designed for precision shooting. While Eric's SDM-R lacked knockdown power, it made up for in rate of fire.

If things went south on our mission and we needed to put down accurate suppressing fire, the SDM-R did the job. Unlike the bolt action rifle, I carried, after each shot I manually had to reload, Eric brought a semi-automatic. The lighter 5.56 caliber round also allowed Eric to take more ammo.

Each of us carried on our backs everything we needed to last us for seventy hours. We brought water, food, extra pairs of socks, batteries, radio, night vision, ghillie suits, and our rifle drag bag. In total, we were each carrying around ninety-five pounds of gear. Hiking the eight miles through the Afghan valleys wouldn't be a challenge. Our unit in the states regularly held twelve-mile road marches under time constraints. Eric and I could comfortably cover a twelve-mile stretch in around three hours and thirty minutes.

With a comfortable breeze that rolled through hills at night, our movement was better than expected. Reaching our checkpoint, I made the call back to base informing our location. The only way command could keep track of us was through our radio updates. Command knew where we had to be and when we were to be there from our pre-mission planning. Worse case, if the command didn't receive a call from our team, they knew something was wrong. If they're still unable to gain communications with my team, a combat search and rescue team will come looking for us.

Fortunately, we arrived ahead of schedule, and Eric and I used the extra time finalizing our equipment. Only the essentials were needed on our last leg of the movement to our firing position. Our rifles, spotting scope, data books, calculator, ghillie, and drag bag. We would leave the remaining gear behind, stashed and hidden at our checkpoint. Taking the bare minimum kept us quiet and reduced our visible signature.

We attached the natural environment that surrounded us to our ghillies and rifle bag. Grabbing handfuls of yellow and brown sun-scorched vegetation and tying it into our suits. Eric and I used the same multi-cam ghillies that were issued to us after sniper school. Each outfit is better suited for the hotter Afghanistan summer climates. Our jackets had air vents cut into the back and armpits. The front of our uniform had canvas sewn into it, making it better to slide across the ground as you stalked.

The eight hundred yards that were in front of us would define our sniper careers. We knew that this was a once in a lifetime moment. Countless lives could be saved by taking Rashmi out of the picture, and it would come down to our mission success. The decisions that we decided to make would mean the difference between life and death. One less bad guy or a missed shot and compromised sniper team.

Eric and I took advantage of the last bit of darkness we had and began our stalk. While this wasn't the suicide mission Carlos Hathcock endured in Vietnam, it was still dangerous. I gave my team five hours to navigate the terrain and prep for our shot. The last leg of our movement would prove to be the most dangerous and put our skills to the test.

Leading up to our firing position was a few hundred yards of sparsely vegetated area. If my planning was correctly done, Eric and I should have around an hour to cover the dangerous crossing area. Crossing open spaces that provide little concealment is a vulnerable moment. Successful navigation of the open terrain, a sniper would use what is known as the sniper crawl. Like a slug slowly slides across the ground, the sniper crawl mimics the process. The sniper crawl, or skull drag, is also one of the slowest forms of movement. Moving when the wind blows to match the sway of the grass, distance is measured in inches and not feet.

As Eric and I approached the crossing area, we paused to take a moment and deveg our ghillies, the removal of grass and vegetation. The amount of vegetation we initially used didn't match the vegetation at the crossing. Having the excess would make us stand out if anyone were looking. A sniper must be forever adapting to the environment. Nature determines how, when, where to move, and the sniper's appearance.

Each movement is exact and precise. Eric, having the semi-automatic, kept watch for me while I devegged, and I did the same for him. I took out my .300 Win Mag and attached a suppressor to the end of the barrel. The suppressor didn't silence the report of my rifle, only muffled it. In relatively open terrain, even with a suppressor, the gun was loud enough to be heard a few hundred yards away. The purpose of the suppressor only aided my team and me. The enemy wouldn't be able to pinpoint our exact location, as opposed to the loud bang if it were unsuppressed.

We took time, making sure not only ourselves but our equipment was adequately camouflaged. Eric and I used elastic tie-downs and anchored them on random parts of our rifles and scopes. While our equipment was spray-painted in dull earth tones and patterns, they were still metallic, straight-line objects. Attaching vegetation to the tie-downs on our equipment, like our ghillie suit, broke up those hard lines. To conceal the lens of our scopes, we placed loosely packed foliage over them. The powerful magnification of our scopes was able to look past the foliage leaving our view unobstructed.

With final preparations complete, Eric and I made our way across the dangerous crossing. Having studied the map and our route meticulously, I took the lead of the stalk. Being fully aware of where you are always, saves a sniper team valuable time. Navigating the earth while dragging your face against the ground isn't an easy task.

Your perspective of the world around you, six inches from the ground, is disorienting at first. When skull dragging, you can't see what lies ahead of you. Instead of peaking your head up to gain a better view, exposing your position, knowing the route ahead of time is essential.

With a quarter of the way to go, I could hear the village start to come alive. The crow of an early morning rooster and groans from the village cattle meant we were close. We still had an hour before sunrise, leaving us with forty-five minutes to set up our shot. Every minute or two, I would take the time to mentally observe the environment around me. Thinking about wind speed and direction and note the subtle temperature change as the sun rose.

"This is it. This is the FFP." I tapped Eric with my boot, getting his attention and whispered. The FFP stood for, final firing position. This would be where we set up and wait for Rashmi before ending his life.

To conceal our firing position, we placed small, narrow bundles of vegetation a few feet in front of us facing skyward. The concept I had in mind was to mimic as if the plant had grown there. Our firing position had sporadic growth of grass around that it wasn't out of place. If onlooking eyes were to look at our direction, we would be hidden behind the bundles.

Waiting for Rashmi to arrive, Eric kept his eyes through his spotting scope on the village. I wanted to have a fresh eye when it came time for the shot and rested my eyes for a moment. If we were going to be in our position for a more extended period, we would rotate between being on and off the scope. Allowing each of us to rest our eyes prevented the eye strain caused over a long duration.

The village, eight hundred yards away, was relatively populated for its size. As the sun crept over the horizon, local villagers began filling outdoors. Farmers were beginning to tend to their crops of poppy, cutting and gathering the tar from their bulbs. After placing small cuts in the poppy bulb, a milky fluid would then seep out of the slices, which would then be collected.

Once harvested and air-dried, the result is the drug known as opium. This practice is common in Afghanistan and has been for thousands of years. The opium that is produced is a means of revenue and life for their culture. Taliban fighters understand the value of opium and where to get it from. Often torturing and harassing farmers and their families for the money generated through selling the drug. Taliban leaders considered it a form of taxation for the protection that they never provide. Around eighty percent of the opium, which then becomes heroin in the United States, comes from Afghanistan. The money generated through illegal drug transactions is what funds the Taliban to fight us.

"Got something!" Eric nudged his shoulder against mine. "Single white Toyota pickup on the road. Two MAM's riding dirty in the back." He continued observing through his scope. MAM's, were military-aged males, riding in the bed of the truck.

Intersecting the village was a narrow gravel path that served as a road. It was the only road that leads in and out of the town. The preferred method of travel in the area was either a donkey or on foot. Whoever the truck belonged to, implied it was someone of higher status. The first week of sniper school, a class is known as ASAT, advanced situational awareness training, prepared us for situations like this.

As described by one of the instructors, ASAT is human behavior pattern recognition and analysis. Basically, the sniper can interpret social interactions and patterns. A sniper must study and be able to understand how the locals interact and function in a particular area. Over time, recognizable patterns and characteristics become apparent. If those patterns or characteristics are broken or out of place, the sniper can pick up on them.

"Looks like Rashmi may have called himself a cab. What do you think?" Eric asked.

By now, I had my rifle scope trained on the truck as it approached. I knew something was unfolding when I noticed the women scurrying inside their huts.

"I think we might have ourselves a party. Wanna start checking and calling wind? I'll track this truck and see where it leads us." I whispered. My heart started to pound inside my chest, knowing this may be our shot.

As the truck focused in my view, the two individuals seated in the back became clear. Still, too far to make out specific features with my twenty-power scope.

"Got him! That's Rashmi! Doorway, near the barbeque hut eleven o'clock." Eric whispered, trying his best to contain his excitement.

I shifted my rifle slowly in the direction Eric was referring to. To make finding buildings or objects easier, we saw what made them stand out and referenced them to what we knew. Eric was looking at a hut with a flat roof with logs of wood covering it. From our viewpoint, the roof resembled the grate of a grill, designating it the barbeque hut.

I immediately noticed why Eric was so confident that he found Rashmi. Intel photos from a reconnaissance team of Rashmi showed that he grew dirty red facial hair. Most of the images that I've seen of Rashmi showed that he also kept a long beard with a crop top hairstyle. The man in the doorway of the hut matched the description.

"I have a positive target identification. Cleared to engage." I confirmed to Eric.

The crosshairs of my scope were now hovering over the chest of Rashmi Assad. My heart was now pounding, making my crosshairs jump and tremble. With each beat of my heart, the crosshairs in the scope slightly shifted up and down. Having the slightest influence on the rifle caused it to change the reticle. Insignificant movements and shifts that occur seem minuscule until magnified over eight hundred yards.

"Left to right wind moving at three miles per hour. The wind is holding steady for, and your spotter is up, prepare to send." Eric said.

I took the time to calm my breathing before taking the shot. We knew the range to our target, and I adjusted the elevation on the scope for elevation. The wind was negligible but would still require me to hold into the wind's direction. Aiming into the wind so that the bullet isn't pushed off its course as it flies downrange. Fortunately, and because of the .300 Win Mag's bullet velocity, I wouldn't have to adjust too much.

"Sniper is ready." I calmly whispered, pushing my thumb against the safety and disengaging it.

The white truck that I was following earlier, pulled in front of the hut. One of the MAM's jumped out and walked towards Rashmi, standing in the door. It didn't surprise us that Rashmi had a few armed bodyguards with him.

"Sniper, stand-by. There's additional armed MAM's coming in from the adjacent hut." Eric said.

Six of Rashmi's men were meeting up with him to escort him to the truck. I could tell Rashmi had been in the game for a while. You don't get to be the guy at the top by exposing yourself for too long. Rashmi wanted to use his guards as a human shield as he walked from the hut to the passenger door. He knew that being exposed left him open for prime picking for guys like me.

Before Rashmi's men were able to cover his movement, and out of my view, we had to shoot.

Breath in. Breath out. Like a yogi going into deep meditation, each one of my breaths was purposeful. I knew Eric's next communication with me was going to be to fire. Everything that we've trained for came down to a three-and-a-half-pound trigger pull.

"Get up! Wake up, gentlemen, boys, and the guys in the Navy!"

"What the hell?" I thought.

"I said, wake up! Last day graded stalks, and our hard time is in an hour."

That voice stood out and wasn't hard to recognize. I've had to hear it every morning for weeks, now…The class leader.

Today was the final day of graded stalks for our class. The size of our class will significantly decrease in size after the end of the day. Having one of the highest failure rates, I'm surprised I was able to get any sleep at all. The last day of graded stalks is what's on everyone's mind.

STALKS: FINALS

Waking up the morning of the stalking phase and walking over to the classroom, you could cut the tension in the air. A short walk over to the schoolhouse from the barracks, less than three hundred yards felt like a marathon. Knowing in the back of your mind that our class would take a massive loss after the final grades were handed out.

"Once you've hunted man, I can and will guarantee all of you this one truth. There will be nothing like it and the one thing that you will never find outside of this career." Sgt. Keller, standing in front of our class formation on an old gravel road, stated. Taking a long pause before looking at the remaining students in the class.

Each one of us looked like we stepped right out of a cheesy Big Foot film. Frayed burlap strands dangled in front of our face and backside. Lose branches and twigs tied into them to better match our surroundings. We've come a long way as a class, and those of the remaining half still had a long way to go. This was week five. In any other military school and by now, things would start winding down. But that's not the case in sniper school. The intensity of the course and what is expected thrives throughout all eight weeks of sniper school.

It was like things were finally coasting along, and we were on autopilot. Week five in sniper school, just as any week, meant more pass or fail tests. This was the week we all had a chance to see if we were the sneaky bastards, we thought we were.

One of the most dreaded phases of the schoolhouse, stalk phase, is what also separates a good sniper from the great. Putting a projectile into something over a significant distance is rush but getting to a position to make the shot is a different ball game. Stalking was a skill that was better learned through trial and error by being out in the field, dragging your face in the dirt to truly understand and grasp the lessons to be discovered. While granted, there was some classroom time learning and review of FM 23-10 manual, a sniper field training manual.

Snipers take great pride in the fact that they are some of the sneakiest SOB's in the field. The general concept of stalking wasn't hard to grasp and, in fact, almost sounded too easy. Simply, don't get caught!

"Class, behind me in the wood line and approximately four hundred meters, you will find your target." Sgt. Keller pointed to his rear into the thick trees. With it being so early in the morning with the sun just breaking over the horizon, it made the lighting just perfect to stay hidden in the shadows. I remember plotting my first few steps looking behind the instructor as he finished up with his instructions.

"This stalk will be graded and will

result in GO, or NO GO. You each will be given at the start of my command, three hours to complete this exercise. If at any moment while you are stalking and you hear one of the walkers yell out *freeze,* you must stop and wait until given the command to proceed.

When you do arrive in a position to take the shot, you better make sure you can identify the target. After your shot is taken, standby until one of the cadres comes to you to complete the exercise." Sgt. Keller continued with his by the book list of instructions.

Each student is given only the ghillie suit that he made before beginning the school, a rifle drag bag, and the nature provided. Once the clock starts, we're all sent out to find our target a few hundred meters away. Mind you, stalks were graded in the deep woods of Ft. Benning Georgia. I had the fortune of attending during the hotter months. Mornings were what some northerners would consider a state of emergency. By four o'clock in the morning, the temperatures were settling at around seventy-five degrees.

Stepping out the barracks door and coming from a beautiful air-conditioned room, felt like stepping into a gym sauna with a constant pool of water on the steam rocks. Your first breath was like taking in a lung full of heated mist. If you enjoyed a nice shower in the morning, it meant nothing as soon as you stepped outdoors. The ghillie suits we wore could easily cause your body to overheat during a stalk. Staying hydrated as best and as carefully as possible was the only way to fight against heat exhaustion.

A sniper's ghillie suit is like the spots on a leopard or the algae that turtles allow to grow on their shells. The reason is simple, it provides them with natural camouflage. Our ghillie suit will enable us to break up our bodily outline, as well as aid us to match our surroundings using natural vegetation. The algae some turtles allow to grow on their backside, we immolated with small twigs and the vegetation that grew up from the ground.

As straightforward the camouflage may appear to be at first glance, the ghillie suit has been around for some time. The first official ghillie suit appeared in the 20th century in Scotland with gamekeepers. However, it wasn't militarized until the British Lovat Scouts. These scouts were Britain's army's first sniper unit to use them during the Second Boer War in the late 1800s and early 1900s.

Every sniper before arriving and processing into the schoolhouse must bring their own ghillie suit. Each ghillie, hand made from old sets of uniforms, canvas, and netting. The classes a few years before mine, students were given boxes with pre-made ghillies in them. It wasn't until the year before I attended sniper school, did they allow us to use whatever materials and uniforms we saw fit. Having the ability to make your suit specifically for you and to the sniper's likings, only aided in his expertise in stalking.

Before sniper school, for hours a day, Sarah and I sat on our living room floor in our home in Savanah, Georgia, getting my ghillie together.

"Not that much! Just enough to break up the outline of my shoulders. Thirty percent of this stuff is all I need. I don't want to be the fake bush sitting out in the open." I touted at Sarah jokingly. We were tying pieces of burlap and jute onto my ghillie jacket. I didn't want to have too much of the manmade fabric covering my ghillie. The rule of thumb was thirty percent fake vegetation and seventy percent natural.

In my unit's sniper selection, our instructors harped on us not having too much artificial camouflage on our ghillies. There's nothing in nature that looks like a freshly pilled stack of burlap, other than a pile of burlap. The concept is to merely take away the observer's eyes' ability to determine the outline of a soldier's body. For example, the human head attached to two broad shoulders appears to be just that when contrasted on a tree line. Burlap, the way that it frays and folds onto itself naturally, takes those harsh outlines and softens and blends them with the background. Where snipers seem to fade into the terrain around them, is simply due to the amount of natural vegetation placed on the suit.

As Sarah and I constructed my ghillie, we made sure to add lightly spray-painted green rubber bands and tie-downs to hold natural vegetation. Once I find the area that I will be operating in and conducting a stalk, I could rip up a few handfuls of grass and branches and secure them to my suit with ease. The only issue is that scenery and terrain change around you. With every change in the environment, the process repeats all over again. Some of the old school snipers preferred to use plastic zip ties to tie down their natural vegetation, but they ran into issues if they had to add or replace veg. They also made the undeniable and unnatural sound of plastic *zipping*.

Having fresh, green grass on your back as you crawl with the sun bearing down on top of you made like a greenhouse effect.

With the Georgia heat, staying cool was just as important as being able to blend in with your surroundings. The only problem is that you're covered in virtually a wool blanket. To counter the overheating problem, I cut small slits in the backside and holes under the armpits. While it did alleviate some of the issues, puddles of sweat still formed under my suit.

"Snipers!" Instructor Nick shouted from the front of the classroom. "Welcome to week two, also known as the stalking phase. This morning, there are forty-nine of you who are still tracking towards graduation." Sgt. Nick continued. The term tracking, used by snipers when tracking their targets, also meant we were still on the path. "This is your final graded stalk before moving onto the next task. By tomorrow morning, at least twenty candidates standing here will be dropped from the class. Focus on the task at hand in front of me now. Get your mind in the game and remember everything that we've taught you up to this point. Slow is smooth, smooth is fast." You could hear a pin drop in the room. However brutally honest he was, those were the historical statistics in sniper school. Sgt. Nick was right.

So often in sniper school, I found myself getting caught up on the upcoming challenges. Instead, taking the time to apply all your attention to what was right in front of you.

Stalking incorporates and tests a variety of skills a sniper must master. A sniper needs to have a high tolerance for discomfort. Having the ability to think outside of the box and has extreme attention to detail. Simply put, discipline is just as crucial in stalking than it is about remaining hidden. The majority of those who will fail the second week will be because of the lack of discipline.

"With that said, I want to go over the layout of the stalk lanes and how they will be graded. While today's stalk will be graded, it will not affect your chances of graduating the course. Today, we want each of you to get familiar with what we are looking for. Everything that you learn out in the field today, it would be in your best interest to take mental note of it all. Tomorrow morning is when it counts. Those who fail tomorrow will have the opportunity to re-test the following day. It's in all of your best interest to pass the first stalk if possible." Sgt. Nick said with a severe tone in his voice. Reading nearly line for line from the instructor's manual, Sgt. Nick explained how each student will navigate and complete the exercise.

Multiple components make up each

stalking exercise. How each student is graded, and what it takes to pass is just as complex.

Each student begins the stalk lane at a remote location deep in the woods of Ft. Benning. Wearing the ghillie suits that we brought with us, we would remain unseen and simulate a sniper engagement. From a controlled starting point, the instructors sounded a whistle that signified that time to complete the stalk has begun.

Six hundred yards away, instructors simulated the targets that we would identify and then engage with a blank rifle round. A blank round is a cartridge that only contains gunpowder. Instead of a projectile, a sealant is used to seal powder inside of the cartridge. When the rifle round is fired, the blank only gives the impression that it has been fired. Making a flash and an explosive sound (report), the wadding is propelled from the barrel of the gun. Not only was the use of live rounds impossible, but there was also the chance of a mishap as well.

Once the shooter fires at the target, an instructor, known as a walker, walk over to the sniper. The walker stands within ten feet from our position. Our targets were the instructors sitting in the back of the truck. It was their goal to try and spot the shooter. There were always at least two instructors that sat in the truck throughout the exercise. Looking through binoculars and forty magnification spotting scopes, they watch for anything out of place near the walker.

If the sniper remains unseen, the walker will get within five feet from sniper as a second shot is fired. With two pairs of eyes watching, every detail count for the sniper. His camouflage must be perfect. The position where he is set up to fire must be in such a way that he can clearly see his target as well.

If all goes well and the sniper is still unnoticed, the sniper is asked to positively identify his target. To make sure we weren't cheating, the instructors held up a colored card with a number printed on it. Each shooter must identify and relay to the walker what he sees. If the shooter is correct, the walker will locate the sniper by standing next to him and placing his hand on the sniper.

One strand of grass out of place or forgetting to paint over a shiny object on your rifle can determine your destiny. This was far from the hide and seek games as a kid. Having professionals trying to find you adds a level of stress.

We stood in the wood line wearing our ghillie suits, waiting to begin our first stalk. My early jitters had finally settled. I started to imagine how I would go about navigating the terrain. We were given a general direction and a distance to our target, along with left and right lane boundaries. It was up to us to make our way to the target the best way we saw fit. The instructors also informed us that we would have to get within three hundred meters from the target. Theses range limits forced each student to push themselves past their level of comfortability.

All my pre stalk work was complete. I gathered up some natural vegetation from a few trees and bushes and tied them into the backside of my ghillie. I went over my face paint one last time, taking away any shine on my face, hands, and neck as much as possible. The goal of the face paint was to break up the pattern of a human face and skin and to make them look two dimensional. Adding a dark brown or black to my forehead, nose, and chin added depth. Using lighter green colors

to my eyes and around my mouth to bring
them outward.

"Good luck, men. Keep what you've
learned in mind and remember to think! We'll
have a few walkers out roaming around to
make sure none of you get lost. And if you
hear one of our whistles or hear us yell freeze,
everyone must stop in their tracks. If we catch
anyone still moving after a freeze has been
issued, you may face a drop from the course."
Sgt. Nick gave our class a final set of
instructions before sounding his whistle,
marking final graded stalk had begun.

We were stationed just over eight
hundred yards from the instructors on the
vehicle. Despite being so far away, the
thought of having someone looking in your
direction dictated my speed. With a class of
fifty, it was surprising how fast everyone
faded into the woods. The first minute of the

stalk, I felt like I was out there by myself. Only the sounds of the occasional twig breaking marked that the area was populated with men crawling around.

Hunching over, using a large tree in front of me to conceal my movement, I began making my way into the brush. Having a time limit, I didn't want to use most of it by starting off at a sniper crawl. I wanted to make some ground toward the target. Having time to set up meant more to me, and what I felt would be the hardest to achieve.

Less than one hundred meters to my front was a good patch of thick brush. Thick enough, that if I stayed low, I could damn near walk to it while remaining concealed. The brush was covered in thorns, wet leaves, a green moss. In any other situation, I would try to avoid vegetation that resembled anything like it. Thorns and vines acted like sticky glue to your equipment and snagged at your clothing. But I had to think outside of the box. Hoping that if it were a place, an infantryman would likely avoid, the instructors would view it the same way.

I kept in mind that once I made it to the position, I would have to be extremely careful not to set off any target indicators. Target indicators anything a soldier does or fails to do that could result in detection. Snipers define these indicators as sound, movement, improper camouflage, disturbance of wildlife, and odors. Getting a strand of my ghillie suit snagged on a thorn could set off a chain of indicators and give my position away.

As I made my way up to my position, I would start to look around for my next place. I wanted to keep a sort of flow about the way I navigated the course. I didn't want to get stuck in an area, lying on the ground and not know where I would move to next. Always having my next move already planned out, saved me time throughout the stalk.

I marked my next position towards a small hill that had an old rotted tree stump sitting on top of it. The terrain in between my position and the hill made getting there would require a well thought out approach. The first sixty meters on the route was pretty much in the open. A few trees stood along the way, but they wouldn't provide me the ability to continue walking.

Ensuring that I didn't get caught up and snag my equipment, I laid in the prone and crawled a few feet. You never realize how discomforting and disorienting it can be when your perspective is only a few inches above the ground. I must not have seen one of the walkers nearby to the left of me, hearing leaves crunching under a boot. He noticed my discomfort as he looked over, giving a smile in my direction. He knew what was going on in my mind. Every instructor at the schoolhouse knew. They've seen hundreds, if not thousands of students, stalk these same lanes.

My sense of direction began to fade more, and I felt like I was starting to veer off course. Wanted to realign me with the hill, I rose my head up to get a better view.

"Freeze!" Instructors shouted at the tops of their lungs.

"Shit! That's me." Said a faint voice, emitting from a patch of leaves a few yards from me. I couldn't see who it was, but one of the students must have thought they were compromised. As much as he thought he was the reason for the freeze, I swore it had to be me. I knew sticking my head up to look around was a huge target indicator. The instructors referred to as 'turkey necking.'

"Take fifteen paces to your three o'clock." The instructors radioed to a walker near my position.

"You know who he's coming for, don't you sniper?" The instructor said aloud in my direction. I wasn't sure if he was talking to me or not. Instead of shifting my head to look in his direction, potentially giving away my position, I remained still.

"Roger that, there is a sniper at your feet. Tell him I can see his right shoulder. That nice pair of white eyes looking right at me are a dead giveaway too. Have the sniper use his veil to cover up his eyes. He needs to add more face paint on his hand too. I can see the skin of his non-firing hand looking straight at me." The instructor who spotted the sniper instructed over the radio. "Tell the sniper he has the opportunity to give it another try if he pleases. He can make the time if he plans appropriately and makes adjustments." The radio communication continued.

One of the reason's sniper school ranks among the best is because of the students' ability and opportunity to succeed. While the instructors had every right to fail the student for being spotted, they decided otherwise. The instructors knew how hard it was to get a slot into sniper school and what it means to the students.

Despite the many challenges and obstacles final stalks present, I went on to pass. What I once feared and haunted me as a child now becomes my protector and dwelling place in war.

Compartmentalization

Each morning in Afghanistan, when on a small COP, forward operating base, I was able to see our nation's flag. Flying just high enough, not exposing its red, white, and blue colors over the base walls. We would raise the American flag at every base I stayed. A forward operating base is built from the ground up, all hands-on deck. Our unit would capture a piece of territory, secure, and make our base to launch our own missions out of.

The goal of the COP wasn't to serve as a place where we could remain hidden. Most of the time, the Taliban knew precisely where the locations of COPs were. There was a rough period when the enemy carried out coordinated attacks on key COP locations. If the enemy gained the upper hand through gun power or numbers, they could overrun a base.

There have been, on multiple occasions, small COPs being overrun. The engagements would kick off with a rocket-propelled grenade at night. Engaging the base while soldiers were least on guard and inflicting the most damage. Immediately after, the enemy would open up with small arms and machineguns.

Depending on the base's ability to return fire to deter the threat, it can come down to size. A forward operating base purpose also isn't to house a company of a few hundred soldiers. With my experience and time on COPs, I was lucky if I could count forty men. If the enemy manages to somehow overrun the bases defense, an entire company could be wiped out.

I could spend anywhere from a few weeks to months living on a COP. In my eyes, it was what being an infantryman was all about. Sure, at times, it sucked, and all I wanted was to feel a soft bed. But some of the bonds that were formed in the middle of Afghanistan are unbreakable.

The COP we would stay in was in the Northeastern region of Afghanistan. A small operating base that house twenty-five of the most exceptional guys I knew. On the base, we slept in sizeable military-style tents that were like ovens during the day. We surrounded our living quarters and exterior nine-foot walls along the perimeter. Only the essentials needed in combat were kept on the COP. We needed a place to relieve ourselves, a place to shoot bad guys from, a place to sleep, and ammo.

At one corner of the COP was a ten-foot-tall, wooden watchtower. The watchtower acted as the bases early alert system. Inside the lookout, facing in three separate directions to the twelve o'clock, three and nine o'clock, were machine guns. Two M240 machine guns and a Soviet belt fed Dishka manned at all times, twenty-four seven. Two and three-man teams rotated out on a schedule every couple of hours. Having someone on high alert too long and you run the risk of exhaustion and complacency. Rotating out guys as often as we did, always maintained a fresh pair of eyes in the tower.

Being a noncommissioned officer, NCO, had its perks. The job of operating the tower was typically reserved for the newer and lower ranking. It was the job of the NCO to keep an eye out on those in the tower. Making sure the guys weren't horsing playing around, had water, and not dozing off. As uneventful as being stuck inside of a box for hours can be, it's where I hung out from time to time. While I didn't have to be in the tower, on guard, I enjoyed the conversations. There are only so many things you can do on a COP to occupy the time. Being around my guys, regardless of rank, was what I enjoyed.

"You thought we were sleeping, didn't you, Sgt.?" A young private first class asked as I climbed the ladder into the tower. Some of the NCO's would randomly sneak into the tower to see if guys were sleeping. The repercussions for sleeping on watch were somewhat harsh.

"Negative! I know you guys wouldn't do such a thing. Isn't that right, Stewart?" I sarcastically responded. Stewart was one of the new guys in our unit on his first deployment. The new guys were too scared to fall asleep during their watch. They've heard plenty about attacks on COP's, it made it hard for them to doze off.

"So? What do you think about being on a COP away from headquarters?" I said to Stewart, wanting to lighten the mood a bit.

"Not bad at all, Sergeant. Nothing too much to see other than the wood line and dirt." He responded. Instead, he was nervous or not, his response was typical.

Our COP was in the middle of a relatively open field. To the front and sides of our base were large cedar trees. In between the COP and the tree line, hawthorn shrubs scattered the terrain. It wasn't the best location to be sitting in, but we could cover in all four directions.

Inside the tower were range cards that designated the distances to selected points of interest. The range cards were nothing more than a hand-drawn, overhead view of the battlefield. After learning extensively about range cards in sniper school, I often passed on the knowledge to the junior enlisted. A range card as simplistic and rudimentary as they are can give you the advantage in a firefight. Knowing the distances to where objects are would allow a machine gunner to accurately locate and engage targets.

"RPG!" A few of the guys yelled out from the opposite side of the base.

I knew what the sound was, but I didn't have time to say anything, only react. A loud boom rumbled in the distance to our nine o'clock. The rocket-propelled grenade detonated in the distance behind us.

Exploding behind us, kicking up fine dust and small rocks into the air. The flight path of the explosive projectile is often erratic, making RPG's highly inaccurate.

Loud pops and whistles filled the air as we were coming under small arms fire. Small circular holes began forming along the walls of the tower as bullets punched through. A surprise attack had been initiated. That's how life was in Afghanistan. One moment you could be having a conversation with your buddies, in the next in a fight for your life.

"Get out if you're going to be in the way!" I said, fighting my way to the nearest machine gun.

Stewart, as soon as the gunfire erupted, hit the deck inside the tower. If we were in the field, him reacting in such a way wouldn't have been a bad thing. The fact was that the

tower was the first line of defense, and
returning fire would have been our best
reaction.

Stepping over the new guy and over to
the M240, I began laying down suppressive
fire where the fire was coming from. The
sound of my gun quickly joined by the
remaining two. Locating the exact locations of
the Taliban was like finding a needle in a
haystack at times. Their understanding and
use of the terrain are what made them
respectable opponents. The rest of the COP
began setting up and getting into their fighting
positions. Every willing and able body that
could shoot actively engaged the target. Out
of the corner of my eye, I saw our platoon
leader, woken by the gunfire, arming himself
with an AK47. He was so disoriented he
thought the enemy breached our base, and the
fight was inside.

"Mortars! Mortars up and on target!"
The Platoon leader shouted over the heavy
gunfire.

Using mortar fire had been a weapon
we used sparingly up until that point of the
deployment. My unit could take on the
enemy, as we have on numerous occasions.
Instead of the risk of being overrun, the PL
wanted to strike the enemy hard early on. One
thing about the enemy was that they were
persistent in their small attacks.

Taliban would probe friendly forces by
attacking them to gain insight into their
weapons capabilities. Hitting them with an
eighty-one-millimeter mortar round paints a
good picture of what we're capable of.

"Rounds! Grab the tube some rounds
and get rounds on the target!" The PL said.
Not using the mortar often, the rounds were
kept in crate boxes at the center of the COP.

Never experiencing one of our mortars in action, I decided to make a run for the ammo. Grabbing up as many mortar rounds as I could carry, I took them to the mortar team. Each shell, shaped like a football with fins attached at the end, packed enough explosives to level a small building.

The mortarman listened to their spotter for a distance and direction and adjusted to fire.

"Hang it!" A member of the mortar team looked over at me with wide white eyes and shouted. Without hesitation, I held the mortar shell with both hands over the top end of the tube. I had never received any formal training as an infantryman in mortar fire. Hang it, meant to prepare another round to fire, by hanging it over the lips of the mortar tube. Being in a unit with mortarman intertwined long enough, I knew enough to know to make it fire. The calculations needed to get rounds on target was what makes them unique.

"Send it!" The mortarman shouted.

As the eighty-one-millimeter shell fell from my grasp and tucked away to cover my ears. The concussive blast as the shell fires into the air felt like being hit by a Louisville slugger.

The round took only seconds before impact. The position we were in didn't allow us to see where we hit. Only the spotter, in an elevated position above the top of a metal Conex container. could see its impact.

"Adjust fire!" The spotter shouted over the continuing gunfire.

The first mortar shell we fired was off the mark by less than one hundred yards. As the mortarman applied the corrections to the mortar tube, I was getting another shell ready to send. I knew how good our mortar teams were from training stateside. If they missed the mark their first try, they were going to be on by the second.

"Hang it!" The command shouted again. "Send it!"

The second impacted its target but did nothing to deter the enemy.
"Fire for effect!" The spotter commanded.

Grabbing one round after the other hanging and firing until all shells were expended. Fire for effect meant that the corrections made were perfect. Instead of waiting for the next command to fire the next mortar, we could fire at will. Five mortars were what it took to cease the Taliban's attack.

The firefight from start to finish was brief, lasting less than five minutes in total. Before the mortar tubes had time to cool off, our unit was already intercepting Taliban chatter. Taliban fighters communicated with each other using old Motorola walkie talkies during attacks. Their concept was no different than ours, except our technology was more advanced. Having the technical advantage allowed us to intercept their communications without them being aware.

Our unit translator, a local, recruited by American forces after extreme vetting, began translating and relaying what the enemy was saying.

"Haman! Haman! Allah Akbar! We have dealt a great blow to the American forces." One of the Taliban fighters said, giving praise to their god. While we hadn't suffered any casualties during the attack, it wasn't uncommon for the enemy to lie.

"We have lost one brother with their mortars, and we are wounded from their guns." Our translator continued relaying the fighters' message.

Holy shit! I thought to myself, knowing that one of the mortars rounds I held killed someone. The translator went on, translating the enemies' ongoing conversation. Going into detail as to how much devastation the eight one-millimeter round caused.

Reports of a few of the men being knocked unconscious as the mortars impacted. Missing limbs of men as they retreated into the tree line. When asked if they were able to recover the body of their own, they reported our fire was too intense.

It was becoming standard for the Taliban to recover the bodies of their fallen. Recovering the dead bodies would look for their propaganda push. After each engagement, reporting the number of enemy casualties was a standard operating procedure.

Accurate reporting meant physically observing the bodies and photographing them with their weapons. In many ways, it covered our asses from the enemy accusing us of murder. A lot like insurance while we were far from primary base operations.

Knowing I killed a man with one of these devastating rounds didn't bother me. In fact, at the moment, I thought it was a career achievement. It was sometime after that deployment before I felt any emotion at all towards that day.

Driving my pickup truck back from a buddy's house stateside, it hit me. It felt like the air in the cab of my truck had been sucked out of it, making it hard to breathe. I was experiencing the onset of my first panic attack.

Pulling off to the side of a narrow, two-lane country road, I got out and tried to catch my breath. I sat down in the grass and leaned my back up against my passenger side door, figuring out what was happening. Not knowing what a panic attack was like, I thought I had a heart attack.

I decided to give my wife, Sarah, a call to let her know what was going on. Not wanting to scare her, I was as vague as possible. All that she knew was that I had to pull off the road, and I wasn't feeling good. She asked me if it had been something that I ate or a sudden stomach virus. Knowing that it hadn't been either of the two, I agreed with her anyway. Having her on the phone and someone to talk to and listen to calm my nerves.

While Sarah was talking to me, I realized what caused my sudden panic attack. I didn't want to recognize what I thought may have created it at first. Acknowledging what the cause was felt uncomfortable. No matter how I tried to brush it off, I knew I had to come to grip with it. It was during the drive that I found myself reminiscing.

The radio turned off, and the windows down to enjoy the fresh air. I wasn't thinking about any event. Random events from deployment would pop up from here and there. Not giving any memory much consideration. Certain parts of the scenery along the ride would remind me of an event overseas, I enjoyed the nostalgia in passing the time. Hundreds of acres of south Texas farmland and cattle set the scene for most of the trip. The smell of cow manure usually wouldn't bother me. I've made the same drive on multiple occasions, and the scent was expected. For reasons unexplained, the smell of cattle and manure reminded me of the mornings in our Afghanistan COP.

In the mornings in Afghanistan, the smell of livestock manure permeated the air. Over time, waking up to and smelling animal feces was a good sign. It meant you survived another day and one step closer to being home on American soil.

The reminiscent smell of deployment life took me back to our COP being attacked. I replayed in my mind the reports coming in from our translator and the Taliban I killed. I never saw the destruction of the mortar round we fired caused. By the time we conducted our after-action report, only shell casings and puddles of blood were found. I knew that I had killed a man. But the thought of not seeing his dead body, strangely irritated and bothered me.

The thought of the missing, dead Taliban's body caused me to think of another dead body. Another dead body that I encountered overseas follow by another, then another. I couldn't brush it off anymore. I learned how to forget about and become emotionless in training and war. The onslaught of emotions I hadn't expressed was the cause of my panic attack.

At the time of the incident in Afghanistan, I didn't give it to much attention. By then, killing was a means of survival and became a job. It also wasn't the first time I killed someone in combat. The first life I took was with my sniper SASS sniper rifle, pinned down by machinegun fire. Through the training I had in sniper school, I knew what to expect. Spending countless hours looking through my scope on the range. Shooting targets resembling live targets or reactionary targets that give the shooter immediate feedback. My reaction to my first kill as a sniper wasn't one of surprise. I knew what to expect. The only surprise was the fact that I hit my target while he was in a full stride run to cover. The imagery of expelling a pink mist of blood from his back and chest didn't bother me. I recognized the impact and moved on just as we were trained to do

In sniper school, students are taught to compartmentalize their emotions. The sniper motto, "Without warning, without remorse," are the words carved into every sniper when he graduates. Devaluing a human while looking through a scope. Instead of at the body of the target, we aimed at the center button on his shirt. In the mind of the sniper, he is no longer taking the life of a person and only engaging a shirt button. The concept benefits the sniper in more ways than one. The human torso generally has a large surface area.

Reducing the large area down to the size of a button can increase the sniper's accuracy. The concepts are more of a mental trick a sniper plays on himself. If you aim small, you'll miss small. The sniper is no longer ending the life of another human, and instead, shooting a button.

The military, especially sniper school, spend a lot of time training soldiers in getting comfortable in the act of killing. In a time when our country is actively fighting a war, the odds of deploying to combat are significantly increased. Without proper training and preparing soldiers for what they may expect in battle, it would be a disservice to the American people.

War is hell. Killing is not only one of the products of war, but it is also what's expected. The enemy we face on today's battlefield is heartless. Defeating an enemy that's sole purpose is to spread chaos and death, takes an opposing force willing and able to destroy it.

Killing should never be a comfortable act to perform, I don't care who you are. As a sniper, we undertake multiple tests to ensure we aren't cold-hearted killers. Having emotion is what separates us from the enemy we fight in Iraq and Afghanistan. However, it may come a time in war where taking a life is the only option. Learning to compartmentalize and deal with our emotions before that time came, was fundamental.

I never put much thought into what it took to prepare my mind for war. After training to end a person's life for so long, it felt like a job. It was a job that was no different than waking up early in the mornings and punching a clock at a warehouse. Emotions of sadness, grief, and regret never came after killing a bad guy. It wasn't until my panic attack on the side of that narrow country road, I realized there was a problem. It was if a pandora's box were opened, and all my suppressed memories and emotions began pouring out.

My only wish would be after noticing my issue, is that I sought help sooner. The army invested years in training me to react and not feel or question. My adjustment back into civilian life would have been smoother if I took the time to invest in my own mental health.

The Afterlife

A short few years full of excitement, with doses of adrenaline to last multiple lifetimes. That's the best I could describe my military experience in as little words as possible. The military molded, shaped, and altered my way of thinking. I made some of the best friends I've ever had while in the army. My service to this country, while it wasn't a full twenty-year career, it's a part of my life I think about daily.

The decision for me to separate from the military was not mine to make. After my 2012 deployment to Afghanistan as a sniper, I decided to give another selection a shot. Again, I had the feeling that I was at the top of my game, and I was unstoppable. I wanted to try out for the elite Green Berets and serve alongside them in any capacity that I could. Distinguishable by their dark green beret and the beards they grow while deployed, they're the crème of the crop. Green berets operate in small man teams, sometimes as few as three men, deep behind enemy lines. They are trained in unconventional warfare, direct action, reconnaissance, and counterterrorism. The primary mission of the Green berets was to work behind the lines. Often, these special forces soldiers trained locals and fought alongside them in guerilla warfare.

Advancing my career by becoming a

member of Special Forces would be the cherry on top. The mission green berets conducted was the pinnacle of what I wanted to do with my career. It would be the closest thing to be a SEAL as possible, minus having to join the Navy. After seeing firsthand what special operations do, I wanted to be a part of the team, even if I served attachment. I didn't want to be the attachment to the cool guys anymore. Putting in the work, completing the selection, and getting selected on the team was the only way to achieving that goal.

After completing the paperwork and physical prerequisites, I was given a slot to attend. I joined a class in the spring of 2013 at Camp Mackall in North Carolina. The initial selection process is twenty-four-days long, designed to determine if a potential candidate has what it takes or not. The course pushes each individual to their limit, physically and mentally. The thirty percent of those who statistically are left standing doesn't make them full-fledged green berets.

Every soldier who is a member of special forces must complete the mandatory two-week selection. Cooks, parachute riggers, etc., all must pass, even though they wouldn't serve as operators. This would be the route that I would take. To be considered a special forces operator, or a member of their community, a green beret after selection, must then complete another fifty-three weeks of training. The year-plus long course is better known as the special forces qualification course, or SFQC, for short. SFQC is where those selected learn tactics, survival, and a second language. After successful completion and years of knowledge obtained, only then can one have a seat at the nation's tip of the spear.

Having my wife's backing and the physical and mental shape I was in, I stepped foot into the selection. There were countless days without sleep, food deprivation, and morning exercise with telephone poles sized logs. Endless miles of forced marching followed by more marching was selections twenty-four-day cycle. The training that occurs during selection was the most brutal training I experienced to date. Special forces selection is also a secret that I chose not to discuss in respect to keeping their secrecy.

On graduation day of selection, less than fifty men were left standing of the two-hundred man original class size. Thankfully, I was among those who were selected and would serve as an engineer stationed in Florida. Granted, it was only a small fraction of the entire process, but I was one step closer. Completing such a challenging course was one highlight in my career that I'll cherish forever. My confidence level was at an all-time high. The new bonds that I was beginning to make couldn't be found outside the military.

Regardless of completing the two-week selection, life decided it would throw me a new plan instead. In airborne school, during my train up for SFQC, I was injured. After an MRI, it was discovered I ruptured three disks and fractured two vertebras. The option to continue was not in my hands as the injury was too severe. Without having the opportunity to continue my training, I was sent back to my home unit. I knew that if I were given another chance without the chance of a mishap, I would have made it.

That's how training is when working your way towards special operations. Being physically in shape will take a person so far in training. There is also a bit of luck that plays a part in completing any selection, as in sniper school. A perfect physical specimen could have his fate determined by a slip on a rock. Accidents happen all the time during training and are bound to happen.

My emotions and ego were damaged, not shattered. I knew that I gave everything I could going into selection. Having sniper under my belt and that was a dream come true itself. I wasn't complacent with all that I had completed before injuring myself in selection. Instead, I was comfortable knowing the person I became. I was proud of the hurdles that I had to overcome to be in the position I was in. With my military career closing to an end, I decided to hang up my uniform for good. I hadn't served twenty years and retired with a pension and a chest full of medals. However, I had the opportunity to serve and do so honorably, and I hold that privilege in high regard.

Fitting back into the civilian way of life was the next objective I needed to complete. My transition out of the army would be the most significant challenge that I never saw coming. A lack of formal education with a specialty in shooting gets so far in the business world. The army has limited resources in helping guys figure out life after the military. You can become so dependent on the military, thinking for yourself can take getting some used to. Specific guidelines and being told what to do make up a significant portion of military life.

All that I felt I was good at was the army. I was trained in the sacred arts of precision and tested in the flames of war. The outside world started to look like a small box from my point of view. This is the case with a lot of the men and women who decide to

leave the military. That military service may
not necessarily translate well over to the
civilian workforce.

With a growing family and funds
running dry, I resorted to working on cars.
Initially, I began selling cars part-time as an
apprentice at a local shop twice a week.
Eventually, I would have enough time on the
lot that I was able to work Mondays through
Fridays. It took some time to pick up the new
trade, but it wasn't foreign to me. My dad sold
cars in Washington for a few years to make
ends meet when I was a kid.

I wasn't the best car salesman in the
world, let alone the local dealership I worked
with. Selling a car every month to a family or
teens after a new license, didn't excite me. The
person who I was less than a year prior didn't
match the Robert Terkla car salesman. I went
from raiding Taliban and getting shot at a

cheap suit I could barely afford.

The rush leaving the wire in Afghanistan wasn't the same as driving out of the driveway heading to work. I'm not saying that being a car salesman was beneath me. That wouldn't be anything further than the truth. The fact of the matter was that selling cars simply wasn't for me. The drive and aspiration that I had in the army seemed to fade.

Accepting I was failing to integrate into civilian life, I was also dealing with memories of my past. Post-traumatic stress disorder, PTSD, as it is more commonly known as. I don't like to associate the term 'disorder' regarding post-war stress. I've never seen it as being an impairment, instead, varying forms of stress.

Post-traumatic stress was an issue that I tried to hide from those close to me if possible. I found myself letting simple mishaps irritate me. Arguments between Sarah and I usually could have been avoided. My lack of enthusiasm and my weak outlook on life affected my mood. Not having control of a situation that would arise would put my hairs on end. Something as mild as the remote out of place would cause my blood to boil.

Instead of seeking help, I diagnosed myself and wrote an alcohol prescription to settle my symptoms. I prescribed myself a dose large enough, inebriation and numbness were my side effects. One of the only things that seemed to make me feel normal was drinking. Being intoxicated, numbed my daily stresses, and I could forget about them. Not feeling anything was the state of emotion I felt the most comfortable. The bottom of a bottle of hard liquor became my safe haven.

The little money that I would make

supplied my addiction. I found myself skipping out on a two and three months' rent to buy booze and falling back to my childish ways. I would delay payments up to the point of eviction, making sure I had the cash for alcohol. The money that was meant for Sarah's and I's future I drank away. I would drink from the time I woke up, throughout the day and night to the point of unconsciousness.

I stopped showing up for work on time and then all together. My days were spent drinking and being angry at the world. It felt as if all that I had accomplished held no value. I spent my military career working hard as a soldier. It felt like speeding one hundred miles an hour, to hitting a granite wall. The accomplishments that I was used to making were halted by my ability to find a job. Being under the influence was my escape hatch out of reality.

Specific triggers would send my mind back into my suppressed memories. Like a trash bag sitting on the side of the road, an aroma of diesel fuel on a construction site, or cow manure in the morning. The sound of a helicopter's rotor blade caused my heart to pump in preparation and my palms to sweat. Our national anthem reminded me of the American flags that draped over the top of pine boxes, containing the remains of those I served with. Potholes in the street were possible improvised explosive devices. Roadkill was a roadside bomb. The war I fought was thousands of miles away, and I had every intent on leaving it there. Instead, that same war would follow me home where the most significant battle took place.

I sold what I could to make ends meet to get by when Sarah and I's money ran dry. It would take the birth of my firstborn child to change my perspective on life. The struggle that I was going through became unbearable at times. One occasion, I felt like throwing in the towel and giving up on life. I had become so used to being able to deal with problems as a sniper. Having no control over situations made me feel as if I had no purpose. My existence, at times, felt as if I was more of a burden. Not being able to take care of my family was a fear I didn't know how to face. I owe the change in my life to give up drinking to my daughter. If it weren't for her being born, I'm not sure where I would be today. My daughter is what makes me get up every morning to try harder. She made me realize that I didn't need to be a great dad every day. I just had to be a better dad than the day before.

<u>Present</u>

The idea of recording myself and uploading it to the popular video-sharing platform, YouTube, never crossed my mind. Those that follow me know that running my YouTube channel and business consumes most of my time. Some of you may know that I own an outdoor company as well. Few know the origins of how everything began.

My good friend, Hector, who I met after the service, placed the idea in my head. Hector wasn't into the world of social media and didn't have a significant presence online. Neither did I. Besides, my life wasn't anything that I ever viewed as entertainment. Hector suggested it to me randomly one day while I was looking through the bed of my truck.

They say that things don't happen just to happen. There are no coincidences in life and occur for a reason. Maybe there is a lesson to be learned. Perhaps, people are put into your lives unknowingly, who have the influence to change your life. Regardless of your view and what you believe, I'm a believer in that there is no coincidence. I think that those who come in and out of your life serve a purpose. At the time, I wouldn't have known it, but Hector has helped me more than he could imagine.

"Hey man, I don't know what you think, but it would be kind of cool if you did videos and shared them. Like a vlog. But cooler than that. You could even throw some military stuff in there if you wanted to. Who knows man, could be a big thing? I'd watch it." Hector said.

Initially, I didn't take him seriously and brushed it off with a laugh and nod. The idea was as comical as it sounded at the time, and I didn't think much of it. I was still dealing with the issues that I had. Being in front of a camera was the last thing that I wanted to do.

It took a few months to build up the courage to record and upload my first video. In the beginning, I had no set topic or what the videos would be about. From what I knew about vlogging, all I would have to do was press record.

Six months into recording portions of my life and uploading them on YouTube, things started taking off. The number of people who took the time to watch my videos began to rise. I never understood what made my channel garner the attention that it did, but I'm thankful. The dull hours that used to fill the day were now replaced with something I enjoyed. Over time the fan base that had accumulated became like a family to me. Sharing fragments of my personal life was therapeutic at times.

Two years into my YouTube venture, I was able to help create one of the largest brands in the fishing industry, Googan. My channels' growth also allowed me to share my love for fishing. Googan now has fishing products in over seven thousand stores nationwide. The process in which it took place was in a short span of twenty-four months.

The reason I share these achievements with you is not to brag or boast. My hopes instead are that they can inspire. I can tend to find myself getting caught up with life's new challenges, I neglect the past. Sure, my history has its dark corners and narrow hallways, but they don't make me.

I don't see myself as being a superhero or the next Einstein, and that's fine. I didn't have to be anything else other than who I was. No matter how much I contemplated giving in, trying the slightest was enough to make a difference. All I had to do was keep moving forward and putting one foot in front of the other. If the high school dropout from Washington state with no future insight can make can, those reading this book can as well.

YOU CAN DO ANYTHING YOU SET YOUR MIND TO